Srb, Lika

A portrait of a small village

By Miki Knezevic

Cover photo: Daryll Michaelis
Book design: Tweaky 100 Graphic Design

To my father, Milan Prijić
and to my mother, Milka Vojvodić Prijić,
with love and gratitude
for all that they have taught me.

Contents

What and Where Is Srb, Lika?

Srb, Lika is a village located in southeastern Croatia on the border with Bosnia. From the mid 1500s, Srb was in the buffer zone between the Ottoman Empire and the Austrian/Austro-Hungarian Empires. Wandering Serbian tribesmen were given land in this area if they would become border guards, protecting the Germanic Empires against the Ottoman Empire. The Serbs were to be the first line of defense against the almost yearly invasions by the Ottomans, whose plan was to conquer Vienna.

In exchange for protection against the Ottoman Armies, the *knezes* (Serb leaders) who settled in this area were offered autonomy over their own schools, religious institutions and local governments. However, the Serbs were not allowed to interfere in any way with Austrian governance.

After 1700, there was less need for a militarized border. The Croatian noblemen and the Croatian Catholic church, in agreement with the

Hapsburgs, felt that Serb armies were no longer necessary for protection. They petitioned that land in the military frontier be returned to them, despite the fact that Serb settlers had been there for hundreds of years.

Several wars ensued in the 18th, 19th and 20th centuries. Srb, Lika—predominantly ethnically Serb—was caught in the middle of war zones and each war ravaged the area through violence and loss, forcing shifting realities on the Serbs of the region. World War I, World War II and the Balkan Wars of the 1990s each left indelible scars on the people and the history of the area.

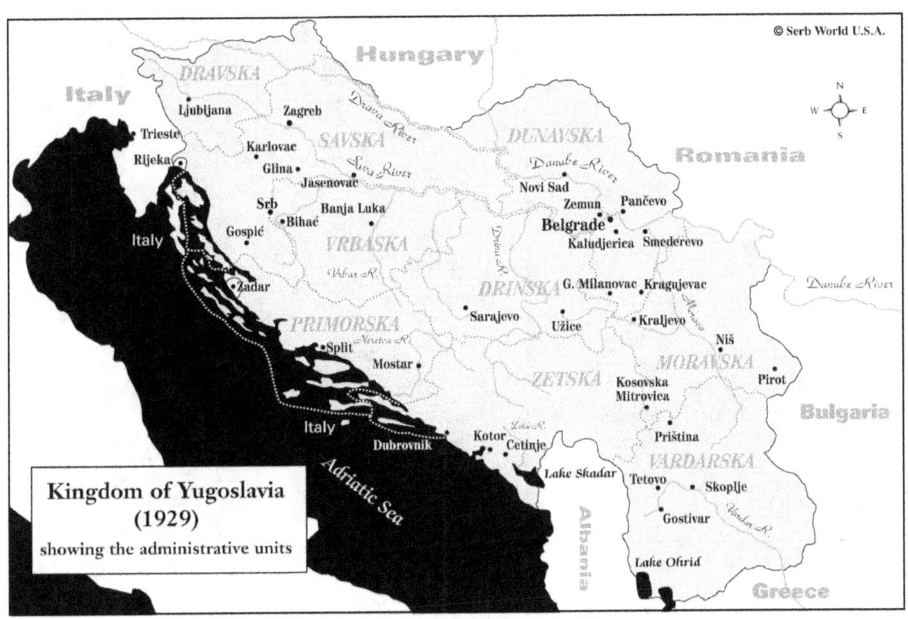

Kingdom of Yugoslavia (1929)

showing the administrative units

Yugoslavia after World War II

Each of the former states of Yugoslavia are now independent countries.

Mother's Side – Vojvodić

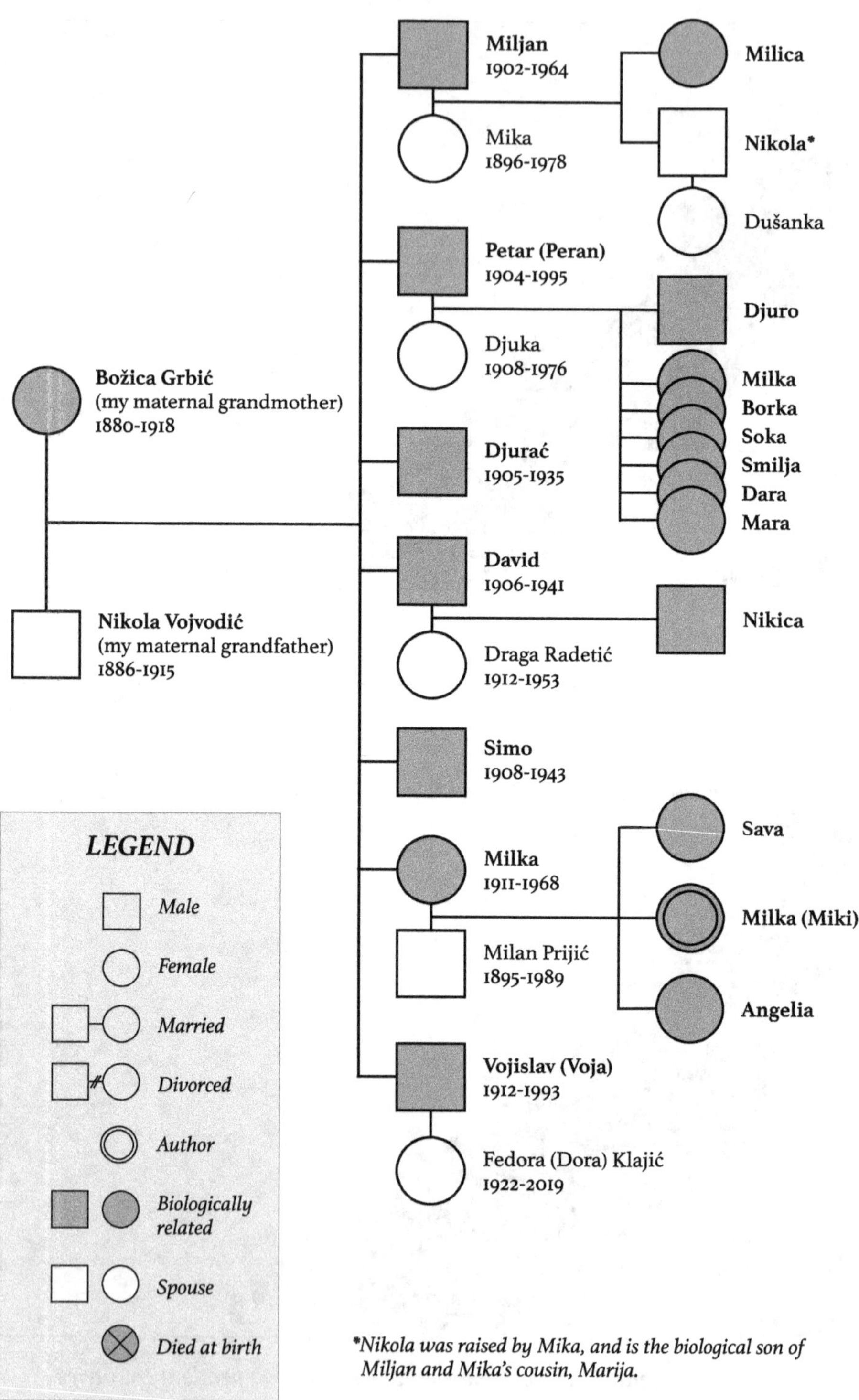

Nikola was raised by Mika, and is the biological son of Miljan and Mika's cousin, Marija.

Father's Side – Prijić

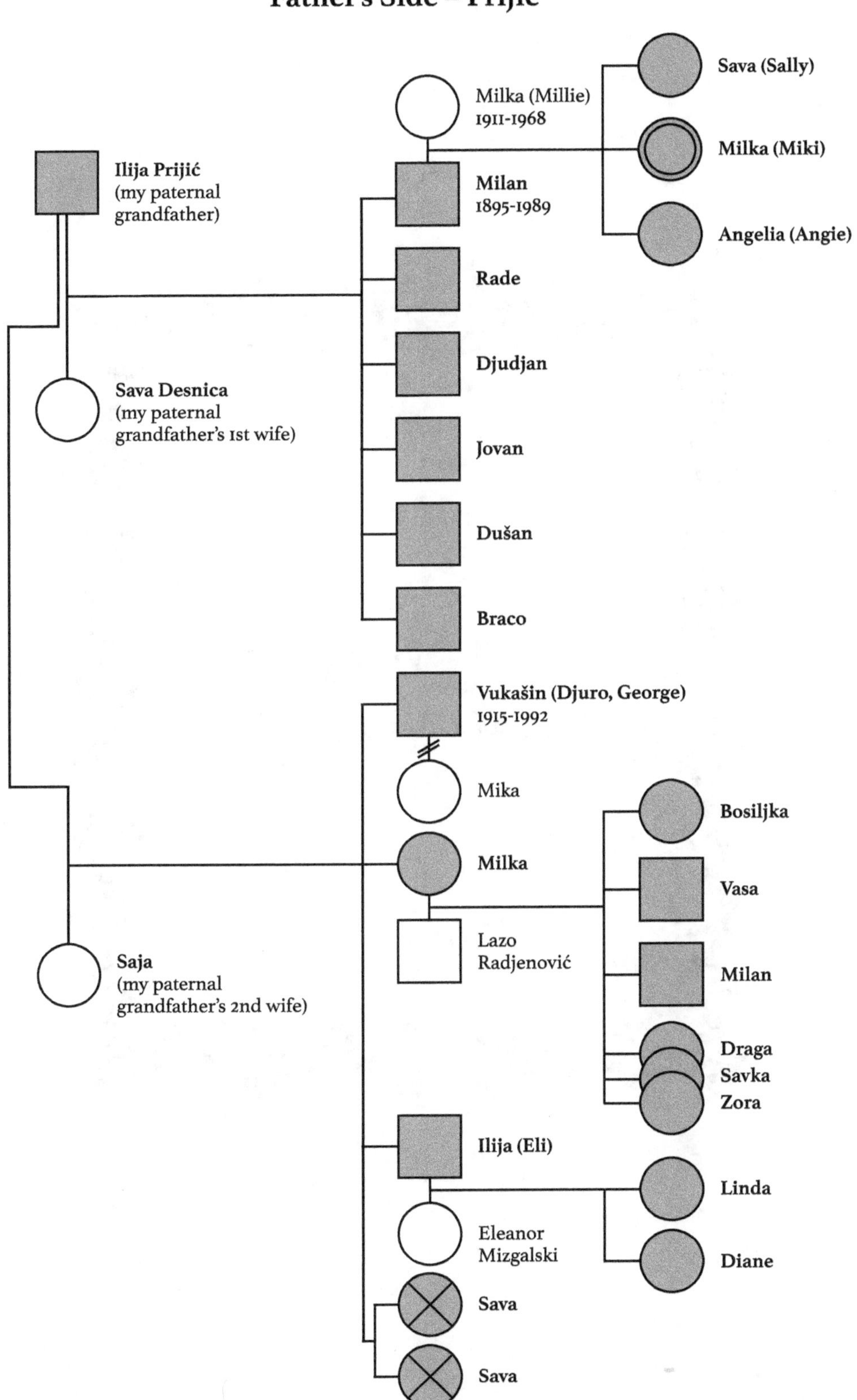

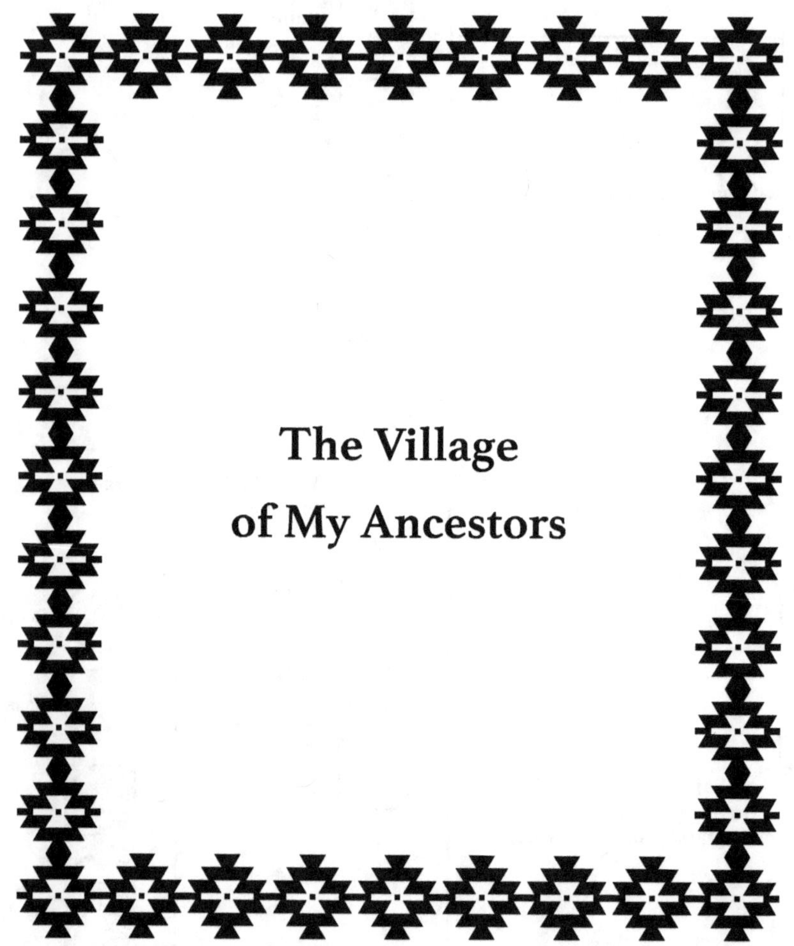

The Village
of My Ancestors

In 1958, after a 25-year absence, my immigrant mother, Milka Vojvodić Prijić, visited the village of her birth—Srb—in the Lika-Krajina area of Yugoslavia. And, she took me with her.

I had heard stories of shepherds singing back and forth to each other from the village's scruffy hills, of hikes to the bubbling source of the Una River, of swims under the local waterfall, Sklop. I also heard stories of the backbreaking work of plowing, planting, and trying to coax crops from the stone-encrusted fields.

Then there were the tales of the ancestors and family trying to survive the hard times and the devastating wars that plagued the area. As a small child in Milwaukee, I remember my mother wrapping brown paper grocery bags and twine around packages filled with coffee, sugar, and warm clothes to be sent to the village to help out after the Second World War and during the early, sparse years of communism that followed.

So, to see this magical village about which I had heard so many stories was a dream come true.

My mother, who had been orphaned at age six, was brought to the United States at age twenty-three by an uncle in Milwaukee who had no children of his own. She left behind six brothers in 1933, the year she emigrated, and in 1958, there were only three left. She longed to see them and visit the village of her youth.

The Srb sign still welcomes people to the village.

When my mother first came to Milwaukee, she met a handsome man, sixteen years her senior, who was also from Srb. Milan Prijić had emigrated alone to the U.S. in 1912 at age 15.

As the eldest child in a family of twelve, Milan was sent by his father to earn enough money to pay off his father's debt to the Austro-Hungarian government. At the time, Srb was a part of the Austro-Hungarian Empire, and his father and the other farmers of the whole area, were obliged to pay heavy taxes. If they didn't pay, their land was confiscated.

After a long and difficult journey to the United States, Milan got a job at a foundry in Milwaukee. He started working the day after he arrived.

Milan worked hard, rising at 5 a.m. every morning to walk 10 miles to work, summer or winter, sharing a bed with a worker on the next shift who slept in it while Milan worked and vice-versa. With back-breaking physical labor, he paid off his father's debt in less than two years.

Over the years, he changed jobs: from foundry to factory, from road building to helping build the breakwater on Lake Michigan, and finally to driving a streetcar. At last, he saved enough money to get his own grocery store. His life was then stable; it was time to get married.

When he met the dark-haired beauty from his village of Srb, he was smitten, and after a four-year courtship, Milan, 43, asked Milka (Millie), 27, to marry him. Milan and Milka Prijić had three daughters: Sava (Sally),

Milka (Miki) and Angelia (Angie). When my mother was planning her
trip back to Yugoslavia, Sally was busy with summer school; Angelia
was too young; so I, the middle daughter, was chosen to go along.

For a girl who had never traveled anywhere, the trip to Europe was
an amazing dream—the transatlantic ship crossing, then Paris and the
Simplon-Orient Express through Switzerland and Italy, and finally,
Yugoslavia's capital, Belgrade. In the early morning, at Belgrade's
main train station, we were met by Mom's youngest brother, Vojislav
Vojvodić—Uncle Voja. This was my first experience with Yugoslavian
relatives and life in a communist country. Adventures were to unfold and
unfold, as they had crossing the ocean, discovering Paris, and riding the
train through Europe.

But the most unique adventure was in Mother and Dad's village, 400
miles away from Belgrade by train through the rich fields of Serbia and
the magnificent hills of Bosnia, and on to the 100 percent Serbian town
of Srb in the eastern part of Croatia. The whole area I traveled was one
country at the time, the former Yugoslavia. After that first visit in 1958,
I visited seven more times throughout the years.

*Different generations of Prijić and Vojvodić families hosted us
throughout the years when we visited Srb.*

My first journey through Yugoslavia was a baptism into the life of a world that I had not experienced in my working-class neighborhood in Milwaukee. What was I to observe, to record in my memory, to feel in the depth of my consciousness?

From the first moments of my mother meeting her younger brother, Voja, in Belgrade, with all the love and tears of her homecoming, we were informed that we had to check in with the police. Being some of the first American visitors to enter this Communist sphere of the world, we were obliged to check in at police stations in every city where we stayed. If you neglected to sign in, your relatives were held responsible and punished.

We were, on occasion, watched and followed. The paranoia of thinking us possible spies was crazy, yet from whispered conversations and over the shoulder glances, we knew that people were afraid. An offhand comment against Tito or the government or a perceived affront to a Communist official, could land you in jail.

I met a female physician who'd spent five years in jail for a mild joke against Tito.

We visited relatives in cramped quarters in the cities, houses that had been divided up by the Communists when they felt the people living in them had too much room. The bureaucrats would count up the square meters, and if they felt there was too much space in your home, they'd move another family in—people you didn't know at all.

Some of the houses in the country—although they were an elegant stucco on the outside—had no plumbing, and electricity, if there was any, consisted of one or two light bulbs in the ceiling. Luckier in many ways were the country relatives, for except in the early restrictive times of Communism when they were not allowed to keep the bulk of what they grew, they had food.

The Communists had wiped out the need for religion, or so they thought. Celebrating your Patron Saint's Day, something unique and mandatory for Serbs, could mean a spell in jail. Church marriages and baptisms were forbidden and could only be done clandestinely and at great risk. Children at school were encouraged to report if their parents were celebrating Christmas, Easter, or any other holiday, and sometimes parents who tried to keep up Christian traditions were jailed. In Srb, the emaciated priest who performed Sunday liturgy in the bombed-out church was evidently killed by the Communists.

Yugoslavia is no longer a country. The wars of the 90s broke up the federation.

Additionally, Srb no longer exists as it once did, an enclave of almost all Serbs. Since the Balkan Wars of 1989-1996, the Serbian inhabitants of the village have been expelled, their homes gutted, looted and destroyed.

And, the last of my mother's brothers was killed—burned to death in the home he refused to leave. Although some of the former Serbian residents of Srb do go back to live, the majority do not.

Two hundred and fifty-thousand Serbs were driven from the Lika-Krajina area in the largest ethnic cleansing of the 1990s wars and Srb is no longer the village of my early visits. Although the Dayton accords provide for the return of the villagers, few go back either because they no longer have a home to go to or because they rebelled during the 1990s wars and are considered fugitives.

I suppose others could write similar stories about their ancestors in Croatian or Muslim villages in the former Yugoslavia, or in Kosovo, or for that matter in many other places in the world. But this is my story, of my people's village, and in the telling of the lives of these people, I hope to shed some light on the tragedy that destroyed Srb, the tragedy that somehow has stalked the Balkans throughout the ages.

Typical house and pyramid haystack in Srb.

First

Impressions

Srb, Lika, Yugoslavia

1958

The train stopped at 2:59 a.m. for seven minutes and thirty-seven seconds in the village of Srb, Lika, Yugoslavia. All who were getting off got off fast, for the trainman, in a flash, waved his nightstick, and the chugging diesel departed into the blackness of the surrounding hills and forests.

Shaking my head from restless train sleep with night smells of unwashed socks and garlic breath, I was struck immediately by the freshness of the forest air. Stars were closer and brighter than anywhere I'd ever seen. Relatives in village garb picked us up in hay wagons and took us to their home. Their cement three-room cottage accommodated my mother and me in a tall feather bed, while the hosts slept on straw mattresses on the kitchen floor.

While my mother slept the deep sleep of long-distance travelers, I woke early to the sound of peeping chickens and cows crying to be milked. Standing outside my bedroom window beckoning to me was my black-scarved aunt, her face a leather map of the world's troubles. But for my benefit, she smiled an inviting gap-toothed grin, made a shushing gesture for me not to wake my mother, and beckoned me outside. I grabbed a flowery robe and fluffy slippers—garb that was completely out of place in the mud-soaked surroundings of the cottage—and sneaked outside to the rendezvous with my aunt.

When we met, she greeted me with a bottle of homemade *šlivovitz*, plum brandy. She explained to me that this was the way to start the day in Srb by gesturing in a drinking motion and pouring two shot glasses full of *"šlivo."* Since I just knew basic Serbo-Croatian at the time (I learned the language better later), I couldn't explain that it was too early and that I didn't drink, so like a good guest, I clinked glasses and downed a glass of firewater in one gulp, just like Aunt Mika. When I didn't die on the first burning swallow, Mika poured me another shot.

Woe to minors who have big hangovers by 7 a.m., but one toughens up in Srb. After a stiff cup of syrupy Turkish coffee and a thick homemade brown bread with plum jam, one is ready to greet the day. So, the 5 a.m. *šlivovitz* ritual became Aunt Mika's and my secret, and we enjoyed our early morning camaraderie during my first three-week Srb visit and in subsequent visits over the years.

*Mika Vojvodić always welcomed visitors
with a bottle of šlivovitz.*

To toughen up in order to survive was the norm in Srb.

Beginning in the 1500s, wandering groups of Serbs who had fled the Ottomans were given land by the Austrian emperor in the Krajina, the Military Frontier or borderland, the no-man's land between the Austrian Hapsburg and the Ottoman empires. In return for a small parcel of land and semi-autonomy, the Serbs agreed to guard the border against Ottoman incursions.

After the Military Frontier was disbanded in the late 1800s, the inhabitants of Srb were required to pay heavy taxes on their land in addition to paying even more with the lives of their young sons conscripted into the Austro-Hungarian army. The whole of Lika and Krajina was ruled by Austria-Hungary until the end of World War I in 1918.

When I visited the first time, I heard the stories of relatives who had fought on both sides in World War I, with the Austrian-Hungarian army and with the Serbian and Allied armies. I was also shown the memorial to those in the family who had lost their lives in World War II, eight on my mother's side, and seven on my father's. All of the duties, few of the privileges. This perhaps was one of the reasons the Serbs of the Lika-Krajina region rebelled in 1990 against the self-proclaimed independent country of Croatia, whose constitution made absolutely no reference to the rights of minorities living in the area. The Serbs in Krajina had lost hundreds of thousands of people to the Nazi Croatian puppet state during the Second World War, and when they felt they were being threatened again, they balked.

For four years, Srb was in the Serbian-run independent state of Republic of Krajina. With the help of NATO and the Western Allies, however, and with the deal cutting of Serbian leader Slobodan Milošević, who abandoned the Serbs of the Lika-Krajina area, the Croatians forces overran Srb in 1995, destroying the houses and killing or capturing those who remained behind.

But in 1958, life was simple. Shepherds sang from the hills, and for the occasion of our visit, with much joy, our relatives were proud to have put up the first outhouse in the area. I helped with the hay crop and we ate thick chicken soup made from freshly-slaughtered chicken. After the sun set, Uncle Miljan took out his one-stringed *gusle* and, under the stars, sang in verse the oral history of Serbian heroes.

Portraits
of
Srb Relatives

Grandpa Ilija Prijić

What do you do when you have twelve children to feed, plus your wife and yourself and you're about to lose your farm to the overseer? The overseer in this case was the ruler of the Austro-Hungarian Empire, who imposed heavy tithes on peasants in its domain. Those who were unable to pay the taxes or come up with the percentage of crops demanded lost their farms. Sometimes for lack of payment, the peasants were jailed.

By the time Grandpa Ilija inherited the farm in Srb in the late 1890s, it had been in the family for several hundred years. He had worked the land with backbreaking effort and forced his young sons to quit school in order to help with the farm work. My father Milan, the eldest son, was forced to quit school in third grade, just when he was learning to read and write.

As time passed, the farm got further and further in debt and in 1912, when my father was 15, Grandpa Ilija owed the equivalent of about $160. So, he decided to send Milan to America to work and perhaps in that way pay off the debt and save the rest of the family.

Besides, rumors of revolt and impending war were circulating throughout the area. The Serbs of Krajina longed to throw off the yoke of the repressive Austrians and to stop supporting their extravagant royalty, who made Vienna famous with their exploits and built summer palaces along the Adriatic coast. Also, if war broke out, all Slav boys in this area sixteen years of age and older would be conscripted into the Austro-Hungarian Army.

Grandpa Ilija in the peasant dress of Srb.

Several villagers from Srb had already gone to America looking for work in the open labor—especially hard labor—market. So, Grandpa Ilija went to Knin, a larger city in the Krajina area, to learn how he could send his son to America. His quest was successful and one quiet fall day, Grandpa Ilija helped Milan, suitcase in hand, into the hay wagon and drove him to Knin to catch the train. That was Milan's first step on his journey to America.

As the train pulled into the station, Ilija, a man not known for overt affection, hugged his blue-eyed son, the spitting image of himself, and said, "Son, I will never see you again." His words turned out to be true.

After two years, Milan had sent back sufficient funds to pay off the $160 debt.

World War I started on July 28, 1914. Grandpa Ilija was sent a draft notice for the Austro-Hungarian Army. He refused to be inducted and to be sent to fight against his fellow Serbs in Serbia. They had just won their independence after 500 years of Ottoman rule and were now fighting against an Austro-Hungarian/German Alliance seeking to take advantage of newly-opened territory in the Balkans.

War had started on the premise of revenge for the shooting of Archduke Franz Ferdinand in Sarajevo. However, some thought this was just an excuse for territorial ambitions of the great powers against newly-forming Balkan states. The Austro-Hungarian/German Alliance feared rebellion in their occupied Slav areas and too much Russian influence in the Balkans. The Russians were traditional allies of the Serbs. With Ilija's refusal to be inducted into the Austro-Hungarian Army, he was thrown into jail. For three months, he wasted away in a cell. With the threat of his farm's demise and family's starvation, he gave in and joined the army.

I don't know where he saw active duty or what his job was in the army, but eventually the Austro-Hungarians were defeated and the farm was saved. Several years earlier, however, Grandpa Ilija's second son, Rade, had followed his brother Milan to work in America. But when the war broke out, Rade volunteered in an expatriate Serbian unit to fight against the Austro-Hungarians.

Rade went to Serbia and joined the army. After the war, Rade was listed as missing in action in Southern Serbia and was probably killed; he was never heard from by anyone in the family again. It's sad to think that, through forces of history, the father could have killed his own son or vice-versa.

Milan Ilija Prijić

Milan Prijić, my father, arrived on Ellis Island in October of 1912. On the train journey from Knin to Buchs, Switzerland, and on to Le Havre, France, he was accompanied by several other young men from his area and an uncle to whom he gave all his money for safekeeping. The men had passage to America on the French Line in below-deck steerage class, thus named because the ship's steering mechanism had once been located there.

Up to three thousand people were sometimes housed in steerage for the duration of the journey, and as the journey progressed, the physical conditions on the ship got worse. Only the barest of necessities were provided. The stench of seasickness, the stale smells of foods from all nations, and the body odors of those unable to wash often overwhelmed the lower quarters. During my father's journey, steerage-class passengers sat inside the cavernous bowels of the ship during the day and were only allowed to go up on deck at night for fresh air.

My heart broke when my father told me this about his journey. But people used to indignities due to supposed class hierarchies often remain silent in circumstances beyond their control. As my dad passed years in America, however, his courage in the face of indignities grew, and he didn't take much guff from anybody.

Arriving at Ellis Island meant suffering more humiliation. Potential immigrants were examined, questioned, and often turned down for lack of money or minor infirmities, especially eye problems like trachoma.

As Milan Prijić waited his turn before the examiners, he stood on the deck of his ship and watched the small boats full of rejected immigrants being taken to another side of the island. On one of the boats was his uncle, apparently turned back, as Milan found out later, because he couldn't pass the eye test. Milan hung over the rail and yelled, "Uncle! My money! My money!" but to no avail, for the uncle couldn't hear as he started his journey back the way he had come. Milan sat on the deck and cried, knowing his chance of being accepted in America was nil, for he had no money to show the immigration official. The minimum was $25, plus money for a ticket to the final destination.

"What's the matter, son?" asked one of Milan's countrymen.

"My uncle is gone, and so is my money," said Milan. "I won't be allowed into America."

"Don't worry," the fellow-countryman said. "We'll take care of it."
He passed his hat, collected money from as many steerage mates as were
willing to donate, and by the time the immigration official asked, "How
much money do you have to come to a new country?" Milan jingled the
coins in his pocket and said with a big smile, "Lots." Of course, he gave
the money back to his fellow travelers immediately, except for the train
fare necessary to reach Milwaukee. This he paid back with his first job.

When World War I shattered Europe and America entered the war
to help the Allies, newly arrived young immigrants—like Milan—were
among the first to be served with induction notices. When Milan went
for his army physical, the doctor listened to his heart and said, "Son,
you'll be lucky if you last a year." He was rejected for the army and often
laughed at the story of how he outlasted the doctor by some 70 years.

With the Allied victory in 1918, the world got back to some sort of
normalcy. Srb now became part of the Kingdom of Serbs, Croats, and
Slovenes, which eventually was renamed Yugoslavia. The area thrived
without the overseers of either the Ottoman or Austro-Hungarian
empires.

Back in the United States, Milan was continuing his struggles and
hard work to make a go of it. He stayed in Milwaukee and from his initial
work at a coke* plant, processing coal into fuel for the steel furnaces,
he moved on to road building, and then to building the breakwater on
Lake Michigan.

His friend, Eli Grbić, my mother's uncle, eventually got him a job at
the Milwaukee Department of Transportation, and he became a streetcar
conductor. Milan lost this job when he had an accident that knocked out
the last horse drawn fire engine in Milwaukee.

After that, with his meager savings and a loan, he decided to go into
business for himself, opening a small grocery store on 2nd Street across
from the Allen-Bradley factory. He stayed in the grocery business for
50 years.

Times were tough during the Great Depression of the 1930s, with
lots of belt tightening, and Milan tried to help by extending credit to his
neighbors who were unable to pay upfront for their groceries. Most bills
were never collected.

During Prohibition, after the United States went "dry" in 1920, he had
also helped out his fellow Serbs. In particular, he lent a hand to his *kum*,**
who asked him to keep some bootleg liquor in the basement of his store.
Milan used to recreate this scene for us:

"One day the federal agents came, and they said someone had tipped
them off that I had liquor in my basement. Of course, I denied it; I could
have ended up in jail. But then they wanted to see the basement and I was

shaking in my boots. We walked down the stairs, and I thought I was going to faint. They looked everywhere with their flashlights. But fortunately, I had the whiskey hidden away behind stacks of boxes under the stairs, and they didn't find it. Whew, the things you don't do for your *kum*."

*Milan as a young immigrant businessman
in Milwaukee, Wisconsin.*

The sense of camaraderie among the immigrants and their families was strong, and if someone needed help, the other countrymen and women pitched in to help them out. When one *kum* essentially became an indentured slave of the company mines in Colorado, the friends from the village pitched in to pay his debts and bring him back to Milwaukee.

And then, whenever they could, the immigrants brought over relatives from the Old Country. In early 1914, Milan brought over his brother, Rade. In the early 1930s, he brought over two more of his brothers— Eli, George, and George's wife, Mika. At the same time, Milan's friend, Eli Grbić, brought over his niece, Milka Vojvodić, my mother.

* coke – A high carbon fuel
** *kum* – Best man at your wedding, or godfather to your children. This is a very close bond among the Serbs.

Rade Prijić

As soon as my father had a little money, after paying off his father's debt to the Austro-Hungarian officials, he sent for his brother, Rade. War was in the air. The Austrians were itching to fight against the rebellious Serbs. The Serbians had just won the Balkan Wars of 1912 and 1913 and were becoming a strong independent force to be dealt with. Being of draft age, Rade risked being conscripted into the Austro-Hungarian Army to fight against his fellow Serbs in Serbia.

The assassination of Archduke Franz Ferdinand and his wife in Sarajevo on June 28, 1914, by a Bosnian Serb, Gavrilo Princip of the Mlada Bosna extremist group, gave the Austrians a perfect excuse to invade Serbia. Milan and Rade were both working at the coke plant in Milwaukee at the time.

Although life was tough for Rade—getting up before dawn to walk miles to the coke plant, stoking furnaces in over 100 degree temperatures day in and day out—he was making money and beginning to adjust to the new country. But one day, recruiters from the Serbian army came to Waukesha Park, right outside Milwaukee. They were looking for volunteers among the large immigrant community.

"Come, brothers, we need you to push the enemy out of our homeland, to save our women and children from slavery and oppression," the mustached recruiter shouted. "And when we push the Austrians and Germans out, we will finally have our own country. Each of you will be given your own farm in our new independent homeland."

Whether it was patriotism or the promise of his own farm that motivated Rade, he took the long journey back to Europe to fight for Serbian freedom along with thousands of other volunteers called *dobrovoljci*. Little did Rade know what suffering awaited him. What his exact path was, I am not certain, but from the postmarks on his letters to Milan and the stories I heard from relatives, I will speculate.

Rade joined the Serbian Army with the other volunteers when it was just south of Belgrade in retreat from the advancing masses of the Austro-Hungarian Army. A decision had to be made as to whether the Serbian Army, which had been devastated by great losses during the Balkan Wars, should fight or retreat. In the first Balkan War, the Serbians had defeated the last vestiges of the Ottoman Army, under whose domination they had suffered for 500 years. In the Second Balkan War, the Serbian-Greek-Romanian armies defeated the Bulgarians, who had attacked their former allies in 1913 in order to gain territory.

Now, the Serbian Army had to decide whether to make a last-stand
effort to fight the Austro-Hungarian/ German forces at Kosovo* or retreat.
If they were to fight in Kosovo, it would have to be on the holy battlefield
where they were defeated in 1389 by the Ottomans. Psychologically and
strategically, some generals argued that this was not the best area in
which to defend their country. The other option was to retreat across
Albania, in hopes of reaching the Adriatic Sea and allied rescuers. There
they could rest, recover, and join the French and English allies in a
renewed effort to push back the enemy.

In mid-winter, 1915, the generals of the Serbian Army decided on the
retreat across the Dinaric Alps where they had been assured safe passage
by the Albanians. Outnumbered three to one by the Austrian, German,
and Bulgarian armies, the Serbs decided they couldn't defeat their
enemies without Allied help. The British, French, and Italians promised
that, when the army came through Albania to the Adriatic, there would
be ships awaiting them to bring them to safety in Greece. There they
would be resupplied and regrouped.

Nearly a quarter of a million people—the Serbian Army, women,
children, older men and boys under 15—were part of the retreat.
The Austro-Hungarian/German forces had a policy of arresting
and incarcerating young teenagers so they wouldn't train as future
replacements in the Serbian Army. All Serbian boys older than twelve
were to be captured. About 10,000 such boys, between thirteen and
eighteen, joined the retreat instead.

I can picture Uncle Rade, with his heavy army overcoat and boots,
his piercing blue eyes lifting up to absorb the huge snowy mountains
that he was about to cross. Some sections of these mountains had
never been crossed before on foot. The retreat was to be orderly, with
different units taking different routes, and rear units guarding those
in the advance lines.

At the beginning of the journey, the late fall weather was bearable—
rain, cool nights, and sometimes sunny days. But then the weather
changed, and Rade faced the greatest challenge of his young life:

January 15, 1916

Dear Brother Milan,

I guess I never realized it would be the cold that would get me: the ice on my eyelids, my blue fingertips, my toes that barely move. The rain has changed to snow, and none of us are really prepared for it. Our clothes are too light; our boots are never dry. I remember the heat from the furnaces at the coke plant in Milwaukee. I used to complain bitterly about it and now I wish that I had just a handful of it. For miles and miles, all I see are lines of retreating Serbs. There are thousands on foot and hundreds of wagons. Sleet freezes on my face, and my fingertips are numb.

But still I continue, for I am young and strong and must take revenge on those who sent us on this awful retreat through the mountains. The women and the children, however, oh God, how they suffer! Every five hundred yards or so, I come across a body in the snow — man, woman, child. I make the sign of the cross over them and call on God to grant them peace.

Yesterday Milovan shouted to me from further up in the line, "Rade, we have something more to worry about."

"What more could there be than this starvation and cold?"

"The Albanians are attacking the front-line units."

"But why? They gave us safe passage."

Milovan laughed. "When could we ever trust them? They are after our supplies, our wagons, mules, guns. They take anything. Slavko heard from our spies that the Albanians got ammunition from the Austrians, including grenades. That makes us easy targets going through these canyons."

"What more could happen to us?" I said, shaking my head.

"I'm so cold all the time, Rade, that I think I can't make it much longer. I no longer feel my toes. And all we eat is mush."

But I told him to quit complaining about the mush. "Don't you remember what happened when some of our guys bought bread in that Albanian village?"

It was just about two weeks ago when Ljubo caught up to me in line. He was yelling and yelling. 'Rade. It's bread! Thick wheat bread, just like we used to have at home. Remember, with pršuta and cheese and sometimes plum jam?'

Ljubo had a big grin on his red face, and he broke his bread and offered half to me. But I didn't take it because

The death-defying march of the Serbian Army from Belgrade through Albania during World War I.

Ljubo was so skinny that I was worried he'd die from starvation, and I was a bit stronger.

That night, those who'd eaten the bread started throwing up all over the white snow and grabbed their stomachs in pain. They constantly ran to the edge of the terrain to relieve themselves, sometimes not making it. The stench was just horrible, just like the pigpens back home. Finally, we got word from one of the camp doctors that the bread was contaminated with a poisonous fungus. I ran and looked for Ljubo.

"I'm dying, Rade. I can't hold anything down anymore." He was shivering and his teeth were chattering. I took him in my arms.

"Ljubo, hang on. You'll get over it."

He vomited again and screamed in pain as he clutched his stomach. I took out my flask of šlivovitz and gave Ljubo a swig. Maybe if I gave him enough, it would dull the pain. He calmed down a little and looked at me with the eyes of one being led to the hangman. The order to march sounded through the mountains.

Serbian soldiers helping Serbian children and civilians stay alive during the brutally cold retreat from Serbia to the Italian coast.

"Go Rade," Ljubo said. "I cannot go on any longer.'

I left my flask with him, pounded the snow off my coat, and turned to leave, tears freezing in my eyes. I walked a few steps and turned back one more time. "Till we see each other again, brother," I said to him. But Ljubo didn't respond. He was curled up in the snow like a baby.

Babies in the snow. Yesterday I came upon a beautiful mother with black braids sitting up against a tree. She had on a deep blue coat, like the Virgin Mary's cape. At her breast was a very young baby, lots of black hair, tiny features. It was like a painting of the Madonna. But it was a still life: they were frozen to death. I lowered them, made the sign of the cross, and covered them both with the coat. Damn them all who make war.

Your brother,
Rade

When what was left of the Serbian Army emerged from the mountains to the plains of Albania after three months of tortuous retreat, the Italian "allies" offered no assistance in food and medical help as they had promised the French and British. With their own territorial gains in mind, the Italians didn't want to see a revitalized Serbian army, which they considered a threat to their land grab, especially the Adriatic coast.

They sent messages to the French and British that few Serbs had survived the retreat and that the few who had were almost beyond help. Not until the French received accurate reports in late December were they able to force the Italians to fulfill their obligations to deliver supplies to the Serbs.

The exhausted Serbian Army, including Uncle Rade and all who survived the long march and finally reached the Albanian coast, later named the retreat "Albanian Golgotha" after Jesus' suffering on the Cross. Allied ships were brought to pick them up and take them to the island of Corfu to recover. Under attack by Austrian planes and warships, two Austrian brigades and Albanian snipers, the Serbians left Albania in French and British ships.

The ailing army recuperated on Corfu, Greece, but even there an estimated 10,000 died of the after effects of the long march—typhus, malaria, diarrhea and pneumonia. The sickest of the Serbs were transported to the island of Vid, near Corfu. Most died. Bodies were stacked on the beach and then piled on barges and simply dumped at sea.

Of the 220,000 Serbian soldiers who started the retreat, 150,000 survived. Of the 30, 000 civilians who accompanied the soldiers, only half survived. Of the 10, 000 young boys between thirteen and eighteen who had gone on the retreat to avoid capture, 2,000 perished.

The soldiers who survived recuperated and rested in Corfu. A large military camp was built in Bizerta, Tunisia, and the civilian survivors were taken to Corsica. In just a few months, the Serbian Army went to join the Allies in Salonika, Greece. The plan was to regroup with British and French troops and push the invading Austro-German troops back through Greece and Serbia. When the revitalized Serbian Army heard that German troops in Belgrade were being particularly brutal with the civilians, they thought of their loved ones at home and couldn't wait for Allied orders. They went ahead and broke through German lines at the Serbian border. From there—joined by French troops—they rampaged all the way to Belgrade, changing the tide of the war.

The last letter my dad received from his brother was from the Salonika Front. He was probably killed in the effort to chase the Germans, Austrians, and Bulgarians from Serbian soil, which the Serbs ultimately did.

April 27, 1917

Dear Brother Milan,

Here we are in Greece waiting for our allies to move north and recapture Belgrade although I don't know how long we will wait. The men are getting restless, especially after we've heard stories of increased cruelties by the Germans, especially the hanging of our men in the main square, mistreating the women, and arresting our young boys. The men are anxious to go home and save their wives, parents and children, that is, those who are left.

Sometimes I wonder, brother, after going through all I've gone through and seeing what I've seen, would I volunteer again? Sometimes I think I should have stayed in America. Maybe the American army would have taken me instead? And one good thing: I could have learned better English. Now I am thinking, with my soldier's pay and after we win this war—and we will—should I come back to America? Or, maybe I will get my farmland in Serbia, as they promised. I don't know. And, maybe if we win against the Austrians, I can ask for a farm next to father's. Wouldn't that be something? I don't know. I will decide later. But first, I must fight.

Thank you for all your kindness, Big Brother. Don't work too hard, although I know you will. I will write you again when I can.

Your brother,
Rade

In 1989, my husband Ivan and I were traveling through Salonika and went to visit the memorial erected by the Greeks and the French to the brave Serbian soldiers killed in the battles in the area during World War I. We looked for Uncle Rade's name but didn't find it. The guard who stands guarding the memorial with a rifle from the First World War, said that it wasn't unusual because many of the soldiers there were unidentified.

Since the memorial was built in 1918, a guard has stood in front of it every day. The guards are from the same family, and the job is passed from father to son. Often people come from Serbia to Salonika to find their relatives' names on the tomb walls of the memorial. They afix crosses, books, flute pipes, *gusle*, and cigarettes on the tombs of their loved ones.

Kosovo is Serbia's broad fertile southern plain. Great armies have clashed there since the beginning of time. Kosovo gave its name to the battle of 1389 when the Serbian Prince Lazar was defeated by the Ottoman Sultan Murad I. This led to the 500-year dominance of the Ottoman Empire over the Serbs. Through the centuries, Kosovo has been the timeless symbol of Serbian courage in the face of overwhelming odds. The story of Kosovo is a reminder of the eternal struggle against invasion, tyranny and oppression.

In the Balkan Wars of the 1990s, Kosovo was "liberated" with the help of US and UN troops. The supposed "independent" country of Kosovo is now Muslim held and is one of the main sources of the drug, white slavery, and ammunition trade in Europe.

Milka (Millie) Vojvodić Prijić

"You will cross a big body of water," said the gypsy with the gold hoop earrings as she held the young girl's hand. "You will marry in a far-off land."

Milka's eyes widened as she tried to imagine any town or village beyond Srb. The gypsy's black eyes narrowed, and she said, "I see a husband and three children in your future."

The young girl having her fortune read was my mother. The country beyond the big body of water turned out to be America. The man she would marry was Milan Prijić, my father. The three children are my two sisters and myself.

Milka Vojvodić Prijić had a hard life in Srb. She was born in 1912 on her family's journey to the summer fields. Her mother got off the wagon in which she was traveling and bore the child on the side of the road. The new baby was given the same name as her sister who had died at birth the year before.

For six years, Milka knew the warmth of a mother's love, even though there were six older brothers and one younger, Vojislav. Milka's father died of the Spanish Influenza when she was four; her mother, Božica, died of pneumonia when she was six. In 1918, during the hard times of the First World War in Europe, the seven Vojvodić children became orphans.

Milka Vojvodić, my mother, as a teenager in Srb.

Since Milka was the only girl in the family, she was sent to live with an aunt. The aunt, who had a daughter of her own, treated Milka more as a servant than a second daughter. Aunt Roda's daughter was allowed to go to school while Milka was forced to stay at home, clean the house, and tend to the chickens and sheep. Meanwhile, Milka's oldest brother, Miljan, 15, was compelled to follow village custom and marry an older woman to take care of the rest of the family. He married Mika, 22.

Despite a difficult and unhappy childhood peppered with bouts of scarlet fever, Milka grew to be strong and attractive. "Your mother was the most beautiful woman in Srb," the village ladies who'd emigrated to Milwaukee used to tell me. "We knew she wouldn't stay in Srb, even though several young men wished to marry her."

One day, when Milka was about sixteen, another group of gypsies in their canvas-covered wagons made their clamorous way through Srb. Milka was the only one home, since her aunt, uncle and cousin had gone to a fair in another village. The wagons stopped in front of Milka's aunt's house.

"Come with us, daughter," the gypsy with the full patchwork skirt said. "You will dance and sing and have a free life."

Milka looked around her humble dirt-floor cottage, the straw mat she slept on, the sickles and scythes hanging on the wall, and the chickens pecking at corn spilled on the floor. "I don't think so," she told the gypsy, "I have an obligation to the family that raised me." Milka explained how she had been taken in as an orphan.

"Raised you?" the gypsy said and laughed. "I'll bet you had to pay a heavy price to live here."

Milka thought a while and said. "Well, I do most of the work."

"Of course, I knew it. Come on. Don't be a fool. Your cards say that you should leave here and have some fun and freedom. Enough of being a slave. Get your things ready and come."

The sun reflected brightly off the mirrors on the gypsy wagon, and the black horses pulling the wagons stomped their hooves, impatient to get going. Milka made up her mind. "O.K. I will go."

As Milka was putting her few clothes into a bag, she heard a ruckus from the barn. The pigs were squealing, the chickens clucking madly. She ran out to see what was going on. "What are you doing?" Milka yelled at the gypsies foraging through the stored potatoes and corn meal.

"Filling our bags, sister. We have to eat, too." A rugged, muscled man filled a sack with potatoes while a young girl scooped handfuls of cornmeal into a bucket.

"You can't do that. That's stealing."

"Sister, get used to it if you're coming with us. We do what's necessary to survive." A young dark-haired boy ran after the chickens, caught one, and stuffed it into a canvas bag.

Milka ran back to the house, hoping by some miracle that her aunt and uncle would be there to help her. She found the gypsy woman in the multicolored skirt rummaging through her aunt's things. "You can't take that scarf. That belongs to my aunt."

"I like this scarf and blouse," said the woman, tying the red-flowered scarf around her head, and stuffing the embroidered blouse in her bag. "Come now. Bring your things. Let's get going."

Milka ran to the corner of the kitchen and grabbed the broom. "Shoo! Shoo! Get out of here. I am not going. I don't want to be a thief like you." She hit the gypsy with the broom as she exited, her arms full of stolen goods.

The gypsies jumped into the wagon, and with a "he-yah" ordered the horses to move quickly down the road.

"You'll be sorry, girl," yelled the raven-hair gypsy with the aunt's red scarf covering her thick curls. "You could have had a fun time." Milka turned back toward the humble cottage, head down. "Perhaps I could have," she said, "but I am not a thief."

When her aunt came home she gave Milka a beating—as she often did—for not guarding the house better. But Milka knew she had tried her best and took the beating without complaint.

Milka had to wait another eight years for the opportunity to leave her difficult surroundings, this time with an invitation from her uncle in the United States. Uncle Eli Grbić, a bus driver in Milwaukee, had married a lovely redheaded lady of German descent named Elsie. Although they got on well, the marriage was childless. So Eli suggested bringing over one of his sister's orphaned children. Since Milka was the only girl, they chose her.

The move was fortunate for Milka as her uncle paid tuition for her to attend school and become literate. She met friends at Milwaukee Area Technical College and at age twenty-three, learned to read and write. Also, she got to know Uncle Eli's friend, Milan, much better. After a four-year courtship, Milan and Milka eloped over the border to Dubuque, Iowa, where they had a $40 honeymoon. They settled down and had three children. Both worked hard, Milan at his grocery store and Milka—now called Millie in America—at home and helping out at the store in the afternoons.

Milka as a new immigrant to the United States.

*Milan Prijić and Milka Vojvodić's wedding photo
in Dubuque, Iowa, 1938.*

Twenty-five years passed before Milka had the opportunity to return
to her village and see her brothers. And, I was with her. For someone like
me who hadn't traveled much, visiting Srb was like stepping into another
world, another century.

What was it like? What did a young girl born in Milwaukee,
Wisconsin, find in those rugged hills? Farmer relatives with handlebar
mustaches. Horses and hay wagons as the main means of transportation.
Clear streams where you could drink the water. The smell of freshly cut
hay from the fields and cow dung from the barns. Green hills and rugged

bluffs. Caves where relatives hid from five invading armies during the Second World War. A water wheel in the river to grind the wheat and next to it, a deep pool where you could jump in the icy river and swim on hot afternoons. The aroma of baking bread, simmering chicken soup, and frying chicken. The songs of the shepherds calling each other from hill to hill. Women in plain black dresses and colorful scarves. Men with scythes slung over their shoulders ready to harvest the crops.

It was as far from my Midwestern, inner-city experience as I had ever been. And I loved it.

The love affair between the villagers and my mother and me was mutual, it seems, for my mother was the orphan girl who had done well in America and was now back with gifts, money, her brilliant smile and gentle manner. She'd sit for hours in the cool kitchens or on three-cornered stools on front stoops listening and crying with relatives as they told stories of starvation, death, and battles against the various armies that trampled their village in World War II. And, at the end and after the war, there was the tragedy of villagers turning on villagers, Royalists against Communists, neighbors killing neighbors.

While Milka was conversing and sympathizing with relatives, I, her daughter, the first American-born person most of the villagers had ever encountered, was off doing other things. My relatives teased me, and they made me work, and they split their sides laughing at the city girl's encounters with Srb farm life.

"Hey, Miki, go siphon us a flask of *šlivovitz* from the barrel," they'd order. I'd go to the barrel, stick one end of the hose in, suck in the *šlivo*, and try to make it flow into the flask. How was I to know that the flask and the other end of the hose had to be held lower than the top of the barrel in order for the liquid to flow? No one would tell me. So, I ended up drinking more than my share, and laughing raucously with the relatives.

"Hey, Miki, here's an ax. Go catch a chicken for supper." Of course, I never had any luck with this or with the milking. I always ended up getting squirted in the face. The scythe was too heavy for me to handle, so I wasn't much help in the wheat fields. I slipped and slid on the cow dung in my delicate American sandals, laughed along with my relatives and carried on conversations with the broken Serbian I knew at that time.

In the evenings, Uncle Miljan would sit on the front stoop with his one-stringed instrument—the *gusle*—and pour out a half-spoken, half-sung oral history of the Serbian people. The highlight of that history was the 1389 Battle of Kosovo, where the soldiers of the Ottoman Empire defeated the Serbs. This led to the 500-year occupation and domination of the Ottomans over the Serbs. The mournful history told of the gruesome killings and impaling of the Serbs, the uprisings, the liberation of the Serbs and the final Balkan defeat of the Ottomans in 1912, when the Serbs again regained their Holy Land, Kosovo. Little did Uncle Miljan know at the time that Kosovo would be lost again. And not only Kosovo, but his very own village, Srb.

One Sunday morning Mom and I decided to go to the village church, or what was left of it. Cousin Nikola, Miljan's son, who was 19—muscular, curly black hair and a mustache—hitched the draft horse to the hay wagon and put ribbons and a leather strap with bells around the horse's neck. The rest of the villagers were to know that the Vojvodić's American relatives were coming through town.

As the horses clipped along the dirt roads, many villagers came to their front doors to wave at us, and my mother explained to me who was who, recognizing some and not others after 25 years. She sat proudly next to Nikola in her Sunday dress, looking to me like an elegant queen. Her black hair was wrapped back in a French twist, and she had a smile on her face. She was enjoying this crazy bumpy ride through the land of her birth.

When we got to the church, it wasn't one of the colorful Orthodox churches of my youth in Milwaukee, but a bombed-out shell. The roof was only partially there, and doves flew in and out of the interior. A few faded frescoes remained on the bomb-damaged and bullet-pocked walls. Germans, Croatian *Ustashe,* Italians, and Communists had done their best to destroy it.

The tall, extremely thin priest stood at the altar in his black cassock singing the Orthodox liturgy. A shriveled deacon in a brown cassock, along with two old, black-clad ladies, sang responses. *"Blago sloven, Gospod moj, blago sloven narod svoj,"* the emaciated priest sang. "Blessed, my God, blessed are your people." Then he stopped and asked our names and added them to the chant.

So, the seven of us and the doves listened to the service, and I must say, it was the favorite church service of my entire life. Because of the fear of reprisals by communist elements—at that time attending church or celebrating religious holidays was forbidden—only a few brave souls attended services.

After the service, the kind priest warmly welcomed us, talked with us, and apologized for not having any food or drink to offer. From the looks of his dirty cassock and uncut hair and beard, who knows if he even had a place to stay as he wandered the villages, giving sermons to mainly empty walls. When we said good-bye, after my mother had given him a generous donation, he kissed my mother's hand and blessed us. The horse's bells jingled on our journey home. Later we heard that the villagers were astounded that the Americans had actually gone to church. Several years later, we heard that our skinny priest had been killed—probably by Communists—as he walked on a narrow path in the mountains between the villages.

Finally, my mother and I visited the aunt who had raised her. As we entered the cottage, the aunt and the daughter—the older woman in typical black, and the younger with a sun-wrinkled face wrapped in a colorful head scarf—ran to the door to greet us. Hugs, kisses, tears, and words of praise sprang from their lips, but I noticed my mother stood straight and proud, not falling for the false adulation. She gave gifts, showed pictures, and drank their dark Turkish coffee, but this visit didn't have the gaiety of the visits to the other relatives.

During our walk back home, my mother relayed some of the cruelties dealt her by these two. Yet, after the tears, she said, "They are old now. Time to forget." She also related a deep hurt, of being made fun of as a small girl in the village because, about a year after her father died, her mother took a lover. Single men in the village often visited widows. Her mother—the beautiful widow with seven children—died of pneumonia two years after her husband's death, leaving the children orphans.

At the time of our visit, my mother was already suffering from diabetes and her kidneys were beginning to fail, a consequence of the several bouts with scarlet fever she had as a child. No medical help or medications—outside of home remedies—had been available to her during her youth in Srb. Life in the village was based on the survival of the fittest.

Milka visited the village one time more, in 1966, with my younger sister, Angelia. Then, in 1968, she died at age 57 of kidney failure. To this day I miss her, but I know that she would have been devastated, knowing that her village had been leveled by Croatian troops in 1995 with the help of air reconnaissance carried out by the United States, Milka's adopted country, a country she loved with all her heart.

Miljan and Mika Vojvodić

He was tall, straight, slim and strong; his face was enhanced with thick, black hair and a long handlebar mustache. She was stocky, weathered and gray-haired; she wore a black scarf and long black dress. The bottoms of her bare feet were like shoe leather. They were an unlikely couple, my hosts in Srb in 1958. Their history was long and sad, yet when we were visiting, their house was filled with laughter and generosity. Miljan had married her when he was 15 and she was 23. The oldest son in the orphaned family of Nikola and Božica Vojvodić, Miljan was obliged to marry an older woman who would take care of the household and raise the rest of his siblings.

In their youth, the Vojvodić boys—Peran, Simo, Djurać, David, and Vojislav—fared well under Mika's care. My mother Milka was living with her aunt on the other side of the village.

Miljan Vojvodić, oldest brother and patriarch of the Vojvodić clan.

Miljan, Peran, Milka and Vojislav lived until middle age and beyond; Simo, Djurać and David died young. Simo, who was a soldier in the Royalist army in World War II, died after he developed septicemia when a boil on his neck was lanced. Djurać committed suicide; he suffered from epilepsy. David died under mysterious circumstances from a bullet wound to the head just before the Second World War came to Srb.

Besides raising the rest of the Vojvodić boys on the family farm, Miljan and Mika had one daughter of their own, Milica. She was a pretty little thing—curly black hair, a big smile, a low voice like Mika's. She chased the chickens and pigs from sunrise to sunset and followed her mother, hanging onto her skirt, to get water from the well, pick plums, and hoe the garden.

One warm fall day in 1937 when little Milica was five, Mika was preparing juicy plums for winter jam by boiling them on the wood-burning stove in the kitchen. Milica was napping on the cot on the other side of the kitchen after having lunched on freshly-baked brown bread, bean soup, and milk. Miljan and his brothers were in the fields harvesting wheat.

The fire in the stove was dying and Mika needed more wood to stoke it. She opened the front door of the cast iron stove, said, "Not enough" and went out to the front yard to get the logs. She left the stove door open so, when she came in with an armful of logs, she could just toss them in the fire.

Out in the yard, the newly cut hay smelled sweet, and the leaves from the oak tree crunched under her bare feet. She inhaled the richness of one of the last warm fall days, and her head filled with thoughts of the jobs she'd have to do before winter: gathering and cooking more plums for jam and *šlivovitz*, picking and storing the apples, pickling the cabbage into sour heads and sauerkraut, and slaughtering a pig to make ham and bacon. She dawdled a bit as the warm sun hit her face, then bent to the woodpile to fill her arms with the logs.

As she was heading back to the house, she heard a scream. "Milica, what is it?"

Mika dropped her logs and ran for the door. As she entered the dark, cool kitchen, a blaze of light stood before her. Milica was on fire.

She quickly knocked the little girl over and rolled her in the dirt floor. Then she grabbed the decorative, woolen coverlet off the bed and rolled the girl in it. Milica screamed and screamed. Then she was quiet.

Mika gathered Milica in her arms and ran like a madwoman through the yard and down the dirt road to the fields. The men, swinging their scythes in rhythm in the tall yellow wheat, looked like a small army of ants.

"Miljan! Miljan! Help!" Mika screamed through her tears.

The working men looked up as they heard shouting and saw a figure flying in the distance. The figure gained in size until a ragged, weeping woman, her face red from running, knelt before them, placing her bundle gently on the ground. "Miljan!" she screamed. "Milica's burned! Get Baba Soka! Tell her to bring her salves and medicine. Quick! Oh God, do something!"

Miljan sent one of his brothers running across the field to get the local healer. He came to Mika as she knelt on the ground sobbing before the rug-wrapped girl. He knelt down and opened the rug. The toddler was burned over her entire trunk and upper legs. Her charred, white night-shirt stuck to the fire-red skin of her body. Her breath barely moved in and out of her rosebud mouth. He picked her up, tears streaming down his sunburned cheeks. He carried her home back up the steep dirt path. Mika followed, sobbing.

As he lay the little girl on her cot in the corner, he fell on his knees crying and praying. "Oh God, please save my Milica. I'll do anything. Please bring us help. Please save her." He held her small fingers in his calloused sunburned hand.

A half an hour, an hour—an eternity—passed before Baba Soka arrived at the door, her bag of medicines slung over her shoulder. "*Bože moj!* My God!" Baba Soka said as she bent down to peel the white nightshirt off the little girl's skin and apply herbs and salves that might save her.

Three nights passed as Milica moaned and dropped in and out of consciousness. They dampened her lips with a clean, wet rag and stroked her hair. Through their tears they speculated as to how she must have awakened from her dreams to the bright light of the fire in the dark kitchen and went to explore. As she drew near, probably a spark or a wood chip escaped the fire and ignited her dress, all in the flash of a second. On the third morning, as the cock crowed, and Mika and Miljan lifted their heads as they lay curled in front of the little girl's cot, Milica took her last breath. No more moaning, no restless tossing. Their little girl was gone.

Mika let out a scream heard across the hills, pounded her chest, and pulled her hair. "No! No! God, don't take her."

Miljan choked as the tears poured over his mustache. His brothers ran from the haystacks in the barn where they slept. Cows mooed loudly, waiting to be milked and chickens clucked. The pigs screeched from the back yard. Clouds covered the dawn, and a cold wind swirled dirt around the front yard.

Miljan made Mika dig the grave. She dug throughout the day and into the night, he, holding a gas lamp; she, digging, crying, calling out to God and the devil, pulling her hair. By sunrise she was exhausted but didn't close her eyes at all.

They buried Milica in a small wooden coffin in the cemetery on the hill. The black-robed priest chanted, "*Vječnaja pamjat.* Eternal memory. Lord have mercy on her poor young soul." His hands wavered as he made the sign of the cross over the small coffin, and his jaw shook as he offered his condolences. No one could look Mika or Miljan in the eye. The weight of their sorrow overwhelmed the hills. Even the birds forgot to sing.

They walked in a daze for weeks. He didn't speak to her; she couldn't look at him. Automatically, he went to the fields to harvest; she couldn't go near the stove. Neighbors brought over bread and cheese, harvested her plums, made jam and *šlivovitz*, slaughtered the sow and made bacon and *pršuta* for the winter.

Mika's hair had turned white overnight; she put on her black clothes of mourning and never wore any other color the rest of her life.

In the cottage, things began to fall apart. When the men came in for beans and sauerkraut after caring for the animals or traveling to the bigger towns to sell hay and wheat, there was nothing on the stove. She lay on her bed facing the wall. Mika had no energy, no will. They decided that another relative would be brought in to help.

One brisk winter morning, Mika's cousin Marija Cvijanović—tall, willowy, young—walked up the path to the Vojvodić house. When no one answered the door, Marija pushed it open and found her cousin asleep under the down quilt in her bed. "Mika, wake up! I've come to help."

Mika moaned in her depressed sleep, turned over and said, "Do what you have to do, child. Do what I cannot do." She turned to face the wall again and fell asleep.

When Miljan and his brothers came at dusk, they found a cauldron of soup on the cast iron stove. The aroma of freshly baked bread and newly ground coffee filled their nostrils. The house was clean and the blankets and pillows had been aired in the sun. Miljan looked into Marija's dark black eyes and said, "Thank you." She lowered her head.

The brothers sat around the big pot of bean soup in the middle of the table and dug their spoons in. Their eyes danced. Conversation bubbled again in the kitchen. Marija brought over a steaming dish of polenta and fresh yogurt to spoon over it. Even Mika came to sit at the table to have a cup of coffee with boiled milk.

The spring was lush and warm. The two women would stand in the doorway and watch Miljan as he headed for the fields. He stood, balancing in the wagon, whip flying overhead as he urged the horses on at breakneck speed. His red Lika cap sat at an angle on his head. His broad shoulders burst the seams of his gleaming white shirt. Marija would sigh and turn to her chores. Mika would head for the cemetery to place purple wildflowers on Milica's grave.

During the restless spring nights, sometimes Mika would wake and reach for him. Often, he wasn't there. "Miljan, what happened last night? You were gone for quite a while."

"I had to check if the cows have calved yet. Bosa is due any day now."

"Miljan, where were you early this morning?"

"I had bad stomach problems and needed to spend some time in the woods."

Marija was also experiencing stomach problems, but of a different sort. She started vomiting in the mornings. Sometimes while working in the garden, she would faint. What Mika had suspected turned out to be true.

David and Draga Vojvodić

Nobody really knows what happened that cool October night in 1940. In the police station in Livna, where young David Vojvodić was head of the small police force that governed Srb and the surrounding villages, tragedy occurred. David Vojvodić was found dead, gun in hand, a bullet in his head.

David Vojvodić was content that crisp fall evening. He'd married his love Draga in the spring, and that summer she'd presented him with a handsome blue-eyed son, Nikica. As he lit the oil lamp in the police station, David thought of his wife and son in their cozy new cottage, both sleeping peacefully as he left for his night shift.

He shook the chill from his body by stamping his feet on the floor and pounding his gloved hands together. The golden glow of his oil lamp filled the small concrete office. David opened the door to the wood stove and threw in a few small logs. He looked around for the newspaper that Simo would have left from the day shift and lit a match to it to start the fire. The newspaper caught fire quickly and burned out, leaving a soft fire on top of the logs. David stoked the fire, took off his gloves, and went to the shelf to pour himself a *šlivovitz* to warm up before the heat from the stove permeated the room. He smiled. He hoped it would be a quiet night so he could sleep next to the fire.

Sitting down on a wooden chair, he looked at the hand-written reports on the table that Simo had left: "Neighborhood mediation over cattle knocking down fence; call for help to get Grbić's wagon out of ditch; break up fight at tavern with two Croatians passing through, possible *Ustashe*."*

David shook his head as he thought about the increased incidents between neighboring Serbs and Croatians. The Gospić and Knin newspapers had recently been filled with events in Italy and Germany, and local Croatians were talking about joining up with Italy's Benito Mussolini to create their own independent Croatian state. The war was already well under way in other parts of Europe, and some said that it might even reach this small area of Krajina, as it had in World War I. David hoped with all his heart that it would not, especially now that he had a wife and young son to protect.

David leaned back in his chair to get a few minutes sleep before going out in the cold to patrol the surrounding area. The room, defying the dampness of the concrete walls, was now warm and cozy. In a few minutes, David drifted off and was softly snoring.

A clatter of hooves and shouts woke the young policeman from his sleep. He jumped up, shook his head to clear it, and went to the door to see what the ruckus was about.

"David! David! come on out!" yelled a familiar voice.

"Simo, Vaso, what brings you out so late at night?" asked David as he recognized the voices of his boyhood friends. "Are you knocking on the bedroom windows of your sweethearts? Or making catcalls so that they'll come out and join you in the barn?"

The two riders dismounted and tied their horses to the trees. "David, we have to talk to you about something important," said Simo.

"Come on in and warm up," said David. "The fire is hot, and I've got plenty of *šlivo*."

The three friends entered the small police station. David grabbed a bench from the cell in back, and Simo and Vasa sat down across from him at the desk. David got two more shot glasses from the shelf and poured *šlivovitz* for the three of them. "So, friends, *živeli*: long life to you both." Simo and Vasa downed the *šlivovitz* and lowered their heads. The fire crackled and the wind blew outside. Neither friend said a word.

"Hey, you scheming bachelors, what's the matter? You two mules can't talk anymore?"

"David," said Simo, "what we have to tell you is not easy for us to say."

"No, it isn't," said Vasa. "But we feel we have to tell you."

"O.K., so what can be so bad? You guys are getting married also? You know, that's not so bad. In fact, it's wonderful."

"Maybe not, David. Maybe not. Not even for you."

"What do you mean?"

"We saw something," said Simo, lifting his eyes.

"Yes, like what? Don't be so mysterious," said David.

Simo and Vasa looked at each other as if prompting the other to speak next. Simo finally sighed and said, "We saw another man's horse in front of your house."

"Liars. Tell me you're lying."

"We are not lying, brother. I wish we were. We used to see her talking to him in Knin, at the market, even before you were married."

"What do you mean? Who is he? What is he doing at my house?" He got up, kicking his chair back. "And how do you know he's not just a friend, that she wasn't just buying something from him?"

"We saw them together."

"Yes, and what were they doing?

"She was serving him coffee and they were laughing. They seemed very comfortable together," said Simo. "When we saw a horse in front of your house, we sneaked around the back window to check and see whose horse it was. We knew you were at work and wanted to make sure Draga and the baby were all right. There's lots of *Ustashe* activity around here lately, you know."

"So, who did you see? Who is this mystery man? Maybe he's her relative? Sometimes they come from the coast."

"No. It's the widower who lives on the way to Knin. The one with the big farm and the two kids."

"Yes, Draga and I often stop to talk to him because we knew he's lonely without his wife." David put his head down and thought for a few minutes. Then he pounded the desk with his fist, raised his head and yelled, "What the hell business did he have at my house when I'm not there?"

"Calm down, friend. Things will work themselves out. Maybe we were wrong? Maybe we made a mistake? Maybe he was just bringing some fruit from his orchard or something like that?"

"Go now. I'll get to the bottom of this. I just want to be alone for a little while and think what to do before I go home."

"We'll be by first thing in the morning after your shift," said Simo. "Then we can figure out what to do." "Yes, yes," said David, lost in thought. "Tomorrow morning."

Simo and Vasa patted David on the shoulders as he sat at his desk, the bottle of *šlivovitz* in front of him. When they got outside, Vasa kicked Simo in the leg. "See, stupid. I told you we shouldn't have told him."

"Wouldn't you want to know, idiot, if you were a cuckold? He'd find out sooner or later. Better he finds out from us so that we can help him."

"Maybe it was just a friendly visit," said Vasa."We could be wrong."

Neither Vasa or Simo had mentioned the sacks of pears and plums standing near the door of the cottage.

"Not likely, my friend. Let's get out of here."

They mounted their heavy, chestnut plow horses and turned them toward the road.

David stood for a long time with his hand on the desk. Then he made a fist and pounded the desk over and over again. Finally, he stopped and reached for the bottle of *šlivovitz*. He took it to the other side of the desk and sat on the wooden bench, pouring himself a shot to the top of the glass. Tears formed in his eyes, and he brushed them away with his sleeves. He downed the drink, then poured another.

A vision of a slim, laughing eighteen-year-old girl—a long blond braid tied with ribbons flowing down her back—filled his thoughts. It was the *sajam*, the summer festival, and the first time he really noticed her. Who was she? He stared at her with his mouth open. She was talking with a group of laughing young girls, who were all decked out for the fair in their embroidered blouses and best black skirts. She turned, looked at him, smiled, and then turned her sky-blue eyes back to the group of giggling young ladies.

"Hey, brother," said Miljan. "That's no way for a gendarme to be acting." Miljan laughed. "Man, close your mouth and straighten up."

"Who's that?" asked David, turning to his brother.

"That's Draga, Djurad's sister. She's been away at school in Knin."

"No, not possible. She was just a little kid when I was hanging out with her brother."

"Well, she sure is grown up now, isn't she?" said Miljan. He winked and walked away to join the other men.

David didn't have the courage to break in on the girls' conversation, but no matter what he did, what he ate, to whom he talked the rest of the afternoon, he always had his eyes on Draga. She danced the *kolo* with the lightness of a fox running through the forest. His heart had never beaten so fast. Every once in a while, she'd look over her shoulder and smile at him.

The sun set over the green hills and the villagers headed home singing. He never talked to her, but from that day forward, wherever his official or unofficial rounds took him, he made sure to pass her house.

One morning about two weeks after the fair, as he was headed into town on his stallion, he saw her washing and pounding the sheets on the rocks along the shores of the Una. She whipped the sheets high in the air and brought them back down on a large rock, washing and rinsing out the dirt in the river. Then she took the sheets and spread them on the grass to dry. They gleamed white, contrasting with the gold of her hair. He reined in his horse and smiled.

"Miss Draga, I don't know if you remember me," he said, clearing his throat. "I'm your brother's friend, David."

"Yes, I remember you, Mr. Policeman. You always used to pull my braids." She smiled and looked him directly in the eye.

"I, uh, I wonder if you might want to go on a picnic with me to the source of the Una? You could ride with me on my horse."

"Why, yes, I would like that. What a fine horse you have, a *šaren*?"

"Yes. Aca is a good and strong horse," he said, patting the dappled horse's neck. "He will be happy to carry you on his back. I mean..."

Draga laughed at his nervousness. "Then when shall we go?"

"Sunday afternoon?"

"I think it would be fine. Mother doesn't let us work on God's day. Maybe we can bring my brother and some friends along. I'm sure Mother won't let me go alone."

"All right. I understand. We will make it a friends' picnic," said David, smiling, turning his *šaren* and galloping down the dirt road.

Sunday afternoon, after church services, a group of six picnickers climbed on their horses and rode up to the source of the river, *Unsko Vrelo*. The water bubbled up clean from deep under the earth, and soon it was rushing downhill playing with the trout that swam in its cool ripples.

The picnickers ate and sang and danced, and the whole time David watched Draga's every move. He was stung, smitten, his body drained of blood and aching to touch this beautiful source of life. He knew his destiny was sealed.

The first time he had her was on a hot summer night. She had sneaked out of her home at midnight and climbed onto his horse. They raced to the mill where the water was deep, leapt down off of the horse, and ran for the water, taking off their shoes and socks. As they waded deeper into the water, the wheel turning behind them over their heads, Draga splashed him. Then he threw two handfuls of water at her. As they got wetter, they started taking off their clothes and throwing the garments on shore. Soon he was kissing her and unlacing her bodice. Her breasts gleamed white in the moonlight before he took them in his mouth. Then he kissed the rest of her body. She moaned into the steamy night as he slid into her.

When she told David that she was pregnant early the next year, he laughed with joy, lifting her high in the air, and they made secret plans for a wedding in the spring, as soon as the snow melted.

This all ran through his mind now, as he sat at his desk pouring shot after shot of *šlivovitz*. He laid his gun on the desk in front of him. His mind was blurry. He kept seeing her, then the baby, then the widower from the big farmhouse. "No, it couldn't be true," he said to himself. "She wouldn't cuckold me. But if it is, I am ruined, a lost man, disgraced forever."

He picked up his gun and spun the bullets. Full. "I must confront her. But, what if it was just a friendly visit? Maybe he was bringing apples or corn?" He switched his gun from hand to hand, then put it back in his holster. "What shall I do? I need to rest for a few minutes…to think." He lay his head on his arms on the desk.

A clatter of hooves and shouts woke the young policeman from his sleep. A strong wind blew open the door. He quickly stood up and straightened his uniform. As he started around the desk towards the door, two huge figures blocked the moonlight in the doorway. His heart raced.

"Hey, gendarme? Are you sleeping? Wake up," said a large-shouldered man with a long beard and shaggy hair. "We have something to talk to you about." The smell of horses and sweat and brandy filled the room.

"Sit," ordered the other huge man with a jagged scar on his forehead. He pressed a rifle to David's chest.

"Stop it. You can't push me around. I am the police officer in this area."

"Not for long. You Serbs will soon be out of here. We're taking over."

"What do you mean?" asked David, moving backwards.

"The *Ustashe*. When we have our state, you Serbs are either out or under the ground." The bearded man, his breath reeking of whiskey, slapped David across the back of the head, then grabbed his hair and yanked his head back. Spitting in David's face as he talked, the man said, "You're the damn policeman who made a fool of us in the tavern today."

"I didn't even work today. I work the night shift. That was my colleague." He breathed rapidly as he thought of Draga and Nikica in their soft beds.

"Who cares?" said the man, yanking David's head back again. "You're all the same shit."

David, through all the pain and fear, began to think of how to subdue his torturers. With his right hand free, as he sat on the bench and the man was concentrating on berating him to his face and abusing his head, David slowly brought up his hand to his holster. Just as he was about to pull his gun out of the holster, the scar-faced man kicked him from behind. David screamed as he fell to the floor.

The two men pulled him up and slammed him into his desk chair. "Now you're going to get it, gendarme, and with your own gun."

The cold steel butt of the gun was placed behind his right ear. Tears ran down David's face as he searched desperately for an escape.

"Now is your time, pig. Say your prayers. You will never see the light of day again," the bearded man said as he spat on the floor.

An eternity passed before David's eyes: the face of his mother as she held him and sang to him; his father's sad funeral with seven small children and a bereaved widow standing in the snow at his grave; his mother's tortured face as she lay on her deathbed giving instructions to the older children; then Mika walking in the front door with Miljan, her strength taking over the family.

And Draga, Draga: dancing the *kolo*, her long, blond braids swinging across her back; Draga, naked in the river in the moonlight; Draga, nursing a tiny head against her full soft breast; and the little boy, his first smiles and coos at his father. "Why, God, why? Why me? He saw his mother from some far-off dark forest motioning for him to come.

He was jerked back to the present as the scar-faced intruder pulled back his head one more time and cocked the pistol: "*Živela Hrvatska! Long live Croatia!*"

David gasped.

The little room reverberated with the sound of one bullet shot off from a handgun. Laughter filled the air. "*Laku noć,* good night, Pig. Sleep well."

David's head slumped on the desk. The two men arranged the body, putting David's pistol in his still hand. They straightened up the room to make it look as if no one had been there. This signature fake suicide was to become the *modus operandi* of the Croatian *Ustashe* in the area before full-fledged war broke out there and slaughters took place.

When Draga found out about David's supposed suicide, with no apparent reason for it, she felt so betrayed by his leaving her that she wanted nothing to do with his body or his burial. She was terrified of the future, stung by the rejection and loss. She could barely lift her head off the pillow, much less nurse a crying baby. A neighborhood grandmother would put the child to Draga's breast to stop his cries.

Within two months of David's death, Draga sent word to the Vojvodić household that she was no longer capable of raising the baby, and that they should come to pick him up.

David and Draga's son, Nikica, at his home in Srb in 2008.

The youngest of the Vojvodić brothers, Vojislav, walked five miles to Draga's house, an embroidered tablecloth in his hands. The snow was deep and the wind bitter. When he got to Draga and David's house, Draga wrapped the baby in several blankets and tied him on Voja's back using the tablecloth as a sling.

"Go, now," she said. "Take him to Mika. She will raise him. He is a Vojvodić. Let him stay with you." She turned towards the wall and sobbed.

Vojislav walked back five miles, the baby on his back. Sometimes he couldn't distinguish the howling of the baby from the howling of the wind. When he reached home, Mika gently unwound the baby from the tablecloth. "There, there. Hush, little Nikica; Mika has a bottle for you. And she has a little brother for you to grow up with. We will be happy together." She rocked the baby in her arms as she sat on the bed feeding him.

After six months, the Vojvodićs heard that Draga had gone off to Knin to marry the widower with two children. As the years passed, she bore her new husband several more children, but rarely saw her son, Nikica.

Until several other "suicides" in the same fashion took place in the area months later, nobody suspected that David had been murdered. Within six months of David's murder, World War II burst upon the village of Srb and all its inhabitants.

*The *Ustashe* Militia was the pro-fascist army of Croatia whose members killed hundreds of thousands of Serbs, Jews, Roma and political dissidents during World War II.

Petar (Peran) and Djuka Vojvodić

Petar (Peran) Vojvodić was the runt of the clan. The second of the Vojvodić brothers after Miljan, he was barely 5'3" tall. But what he lacked in height, he made up in feistiness.

Whenever I met Uncle Peran, from the first encounter and on, when I asked him how he was doing, he'd make a fist, pound himself hard on the chest and say, "Umph" to indicate his toughness. Then he'd grin, showing only two large front teeth on top, and all his teeth on the bottom except for the two lower front ones. His smile fit together like a jigsaw puzzle.

While all the Vojvodić brothers lived in the house on top of the hill, and Miljan and Mika took care of them, the family worked their land together. But when Peran married his green-eyed wife, Djuka, right before World War II, the two oldest Vojvodić brothers divided the land between them. The rest of the sons in the family were expected to learn a trade and not work the land.

Peran and Djuka built a small, simple cottage at the bottom of the hill on the Vojvodić property and worked the land across the road.

The house had a packed-down dirt floor, cement walls, and a wood-burning stove with a super-size metal kettle on it. When a fire was built underneath

Uncle Peran playing the gusle in front of his home.

the kettle, batches of beans and cabbage were cooked for meals. Substantial food was necessary since Peran and Djuka had seven children, one son and six daughters.

Djuka and Peran Vojvodić, 1958.

While Peran and Djuka slept on a primitive wooden bed, the children—covered with feather quilts—slept on straw mats on the floor. On the other side of the wall, the cattle slept, a common practice to provide extra warmth in the house during the freezing cold winter.

During World War II, when he wasn't tending his crops, Peran was out in the forest and hills with the rest of the village men fighting the various armies that swept through Srb. Their weapons ranged from pitchforks to rifles as they fought the motorized, disciplined Germans passing through on tanks and motorcycles; the Italians in their disorganized, but nonetheless cruel raids; and the Croatian *Ustashe*, who wanted to take the territory for their own and fought the most brutally. Before the war was over, a civil war had erupted between the Serbian Royalists under General Draža Mihailović and the Partisans under Josip Broz—Tito.

While both Royalists and Communists fought the Nazis, rivalries and infighting for postwar power shattered the unity of cities, towns, and villages throughout Yugoslavia. As the war progressed, the Allies decided to back Tito's Partisans, and eventually Tito came to power. Many people in Srb had become Partisans during the war and later joined Tito's Communist party. Although Peran was a fierce fighter, he never joined any political group, and after the war, he returned to simple farming.

The years after the war and until the mid-1960s were extremely difficult and meager for the people of Srb and for the people of Yugoslavia in general. Tito's fist was tight, holding freedom and individual economic advancement in check. Many extrajudicial executions of supposed "enemies of the state" took place. Yugoslavs struggled under a police state where an off-hand remark could bring a prison sentence, and where the state either collectivized your farm or took a portion of your crops. During these years, my mother and dad in Milwaukee sent many packages with clothes, shoes, sugar, cooking oil, and coffee to their relatives.

In 1956, some monetary relief was felt at least by my mother's relatives in Srb. Uncle Eli Grbić, my great uncle who brought my mother to America, died, leaving a total of $158,000 to my mother in America and his nephews in Yugoslavia. This inheritance not only made possible my mother's and my trip to Yugoslavia in 1958, but also enabled a variety of improvements in the lives of those who received their shares of the inheritance in the "Old Country."

Uncle Peran used his money to improve his meager home and to build a fence between his property and his brother Miljan's. The fence led to hard feelings between the brothers that persisted for years.

When my mother and I visited in 1958, Uncle Peran and Djuka's home still had dirt floors and no indoor plumbing. This was typical for most houses at the time. Well water was used for drinking and cooking, and the woods were used for sanitary purposes. Plumbing didn't come in until the late 1970s, early 80s. Electricity arrived in the form of one light bulb that hung from the ceiling and lit the main kitchen-dining room. Candles and kerosene lamps lit the rest of the house, which was in the process of being enlarged.

Visiting Uncle Peran always meant a trip behind the outside door to the *šlivovitz* barrel. Serbian villagers pride themselves on their homemade *šlivo*, and wherever you visit you have to say, "That's the best *šlivovitz* I've ever tasted." After visiting three or four relatives' homes in a day, you begin either to believe your compliments or not to care, longing only to stick the top of your skull in the cool Una River.

At Peran and Djuka's, we had chicken soup made from the barnyard chicken whose neck had been wrung by Djuka that morning; crisp, baked chicken; a salad of garden-fresh tomatoes, onions, and peppers; hot, dark bread baked in the wood-burning stove and sweet Turkish coffee.

Djuka hung around in the background and served us, smiling shyly at the compliments given her by the American relatives. A variety of green-eyed cousins either joined us at the table or helped their mother.

After dinner, Peran sat on the front porch playing the *gusle* and singing monotonic epic poetry, passed orally and musically through the generations.

I made visits to Srb in the 1960s, 70s, 80s, and 90s, with the last in 2008. Sometime in the 1980s, after Djuka died, Peran moved to a separate room built for him at the back of his house. He had given the larger front portion to his son and his family. Often, Peran squabbled with his children or one of his brothers or neighbors. He called his son at the front of the house "my neighbor" and had little to do with him for a long time.

As feisty and cantankerous as he could be, his children always took care of him, bringing food and water to the old man at each meal. He worked the fields til his late eighties, and when we'd come to visit, I with my husband and children on later trips, one of Peran's grandchildren always had to run to the fields to get her grandpa. He'd come sauntering down the road, a black beret on his head, his coat on one shoulder and his scythe on the other.

Peran's one room held a bed, a table with a porcelain bowl with water for washing hands and face, and a clothes chest, which, in Peran's case, held very few clothes, and a barrel of *šlivovitz*.

When we'd visit, he'd have us sit on the bed or milking stools brought in from the barn, and he'd happily siphon the *šlivovitz* into a carafe to treat his guests. His daughter-in-law would appear from the front of the house with a plate of *pršuta* and *basa*—a mild, white, squeaky cheese. Peran would regale us with stories of the village, laugh heartily at his own jokes, and smile his gap-toothed grin. The times when the American relatives visited the village were healing times and during these visits, Peran was often invited to family gatherings as an extra dinner guest.

Uncle Peran's finest and worst moment came in 1994. Old and partially blind, Peran had not been able to participate in the war leading to the dissolution of Yugoslavia. It had started with the breaking away of Slovenia, and then Croatia, and the civil war in Bosnia and Krajina between the Serbs, Muslims, and Croatians. For four years, the Serbs of Lika and Krajina had had a self-governed republic—Srpksa Republika Krajina—independent of control by Yugoslavia or Croatia.

Then one morning the bombing started. NATO had given the coordinates, and retired American generals gave strategic help to the Croatian Army in order to destroy the independent Serbian republic and drive the Serbs from the land where they had lived for more than 500 years.

"Come on, *Djedo*, we have to leave," said Peran's son, Djuro, as the planes flew overhead and bombs and gunfire could be heard in the distance.

"*Gjde čemo*? Where are we going to go?" demanded Peran.

"I've tied the wagon to the tractor, and we must leave the area with what we can get away with. The *Ustashe* are coming again."

"No, we beat them in the other war."

"They are back. We must go. Time is short."

"My time is short anyway. I'm too old to run." Peran folded his arms and sat stiffly on the bed.

"*Tata*, come."

"Give me your hand, son. I will not go. I will stay in my house. They didn't get me in the last war, so let them take me now."

Djuro's wife, son, and daughter entered the little back room and yelled, "Come on *Djedo* Peran! Come on, Djuro! We have to leave. The tanks are coming."

"Go! Get out! God go with you. Save yourselves. I will not leave before the enemy. I will not be a burden to you. Let them come." Peran shooed his son away.

The old man sat on his bed holding his cane, his beret cocked off to the side, his blank stare still following the light. "You are as stubborn as ever, *Tata*," said Djuro. "I wish you well." He kissed the old man on both cheeks, and at that moment, all past quarrels were forgotten. Djuro's wife and children did the same.

"You too, son," he said, "and good luck."

Jets roared overhead and the sounds of braying cattle; frantic, clucking chickens; tractor and car engines, and panicked human shouting filled the air. Then the village convoy pulled away.

In the distance Peran heard the familiar sound of exploding bombs. He slowly got up and felt his way to the barrel and siphoned the *šlivovitz* into his carafe. "Ahh-h-h," he said as the strong liquor burned his chest on its way down. Then he sat and waited, singing to himself the ancient histories learned by ear.

The clamorous roar of moving tanks and jeep convoys broke the silence about half an hour later. Peran already noted the acrid smell of something burning.

"Anybody in there?" a loud voice yelled from outside Peran's door.

"I'm here, you swine. Come and get me."

A uniformed soldier lifted his heavy boot and kicked open the door. "Who's calling me a swine?"

The soldier laughed when he saw the little old man sitting on the bed. "Hey guys, look at this. Our brave general over here dares to challenge us."

Two others came to the door, stared at Peran and laughed. "We're burning your house, old man, like we burned the other houses in the village. You can come out or you can stay and be cooked like a lamb on the spit. Sunday dinner."

Peran sat on the bed and looked straight ahead, seeing only shadows in his clouded eyes. "I will not leave my home and my land. I didn't leave in the last war and I will not leave now."

"Okay then, old man, burn," the mustached soldier said, as he saluted, clicked his heels together, laughed, and walked out the door.

One of the other soldiers spilled gasoline around the door of the house. Then the three stood back. Another lit a torch. As they backed off further, the young soldier flung the torch at Peran's door. The house and Peran were history in a matter of minutes.

As the convoys left Krajina, the Croatian Army strafed the departing masses. Over 300 Serbs were killed in the exodus, and 250,000 left homeless in the largest "ethnic cleansing" of the war leading to the breakup of Yugoslavia.

Peran and Djuka Vojvodić and family.

*Two of my aunts from Srb, Milka Prijić Radjenović
and Mika Vojovdić, 1958.*

Milka Prijić Radjenović

On that cold, gray morning in the forest surrounding Srb—
January 9, 1943—Milka moaned quietly, then at times sobbed openly.
The baby was on its way. She wasn't crying because of the labor pains,
after all, this was her sixth child; she was crying for the pain of what
life had already dealt her, and the uncertainty of what was to come.

As she lay on the bed of pine branches and dried leaves in a hollow
of snow, she heard her other children crying in the distance. "I'll be
there soon, babies. I just have to finish," she said as loudly as she could,
knowing that the children couldn't hear her over the howling of the wind.

Milka's oldest daughter, Bosa, held her hand and shouted to the
children. "*Ćuti!* Be quiet! Leave mother alone. She'll be finished in a little
while. Quiet, you babies. The Germans will hear us." Bosa turned back to
her mother and squeezed her hand tightly. "So sorry, Mama. I'm so crazy.
I'm making more noise than the kids."

Milka stopped her crying, realizing how hard this must be on her
barely teenage daughter, having to help her mother deliver a brother or
sister. "Calm down, dear," she said. "It will be over soon, and I will take
care of the other little ones."

As Milka lay in the waves of labor pains, she thought of how her
husband would have loved to have seen his last child. The loud knock
at the door two days ago on Christmas Day, January 7th, had sealed the
family's fate. Milka thought it was perhaps a neighbor bringing much
needed firewood or, in the worst-case scenario, the Germans. But she
hadn't heard the dreaded motorcycles of the men of the Third Reich or
the roaring of the tanks as they crushed the trees in their path. And if it
were the Germans, then there would be the shouts, commands: "Come
out of the house with your hands up!"

Milka and the children huddled on the bed, hugging each other.
The knock became louder and more persistent. "Milka, are you in there?
Simo here."

"Simo, is that you? I'm coming." She gently laid the two children she
had in her arms on the bed and moved her bulky, pregnant body off the
bed. She slipped her tiny swollen feet into an old pair of rubber boots
and clumped towards the door.

"Simo?"

"Come on, Milka. Yes, it's me. Open up. Quick!"

Milka unbolted the heavy wooden door. A strong gust of wind and
snow pushed her back as Simo burst into the house; his head was bent,

and his shoulders were slumped. As he lifted his head, she looked into his frightened, sad eyes and knew something was wrong. "Simo, *šta je?*"

"They got him," Simo said quietly so as not to startle the children huddled on the bed.

"Who?"

"Lazo."

"Lazo? No! Don't tell me! I won't believe it. He's what? Injured? A little hurt?"

"Lazo is dead. Shot through the chest by a German sniper. And they're moving in. The Germans. Take the kids and run to the forest."

"But where is he, my Lazo? I must see him."

"We buried him quickly where he fell. We'll look for him after the Germans go through. No time now for ceremonies." As quickly as he had arrived, Simo left and slammed the door.

Milka dropped to her knees. She felt the baby that was never to see his father kick violently inside of her. She wanted to stay on the floor, collapse, faint.

"Mama! Mama! What is it?"

Milka heard the calls of her children, momentarily forgotten on the bed. "Children, children, hurry. We must run to the forest. The Germans are coming," she shouted, as she dragged her pregnant bulk off the floor.

"And *Tata?*" yelled her son Vasa. "Where is *Tata?* Is he coming with us?"

"*Tata* is hurt. He will get some help. He will come later. Grab your shoes and heavy coats. Don't forget your mittens and heavy socks. Put on as many clothes as you can stand. And take the quilts and sheets. Don't forget the sheets. We must hurry. I will bring some bread and milk. Vaso, run fast to the barn and bring the *pršuta.*"

"But what about Christmas, Mama?" cried Bosa, twirling her pigtails in her fingers.

"The Germans are coming. Christmas must wait."

So instead of the Christmas pig on the spit, and the burning of the yule log, with laughter and merriment led by *Tata*, the small, bundled family made a dash for the density of the dark and snowy forest.

As a light snow began to fall again, a wave of great pain engulfed Milka and jackknifed her body. "Lift the blanket, Bosa. The baby is coming."

The frightened young girl lifted the blanket as a blackish moist head began to emerge from her mother's body. She started to cry. "Mama, what shall I do?"

"Calm down, child. You must take the baby as it comes out. It will be out in a minute. Oh-h-h, it's coming." With a cry and then a great sigh of relief as if an earthquake had subsided, Milka gave birth to her baby. Hearty cries came from the tiny body held by Bosa, and a cord and after birth hung over one of her arms. "Here, child, give him to me so I can cover him with my shawl," said Milka after her panting had subsided. "And hand me the knife; I must cut the cord. Is it a boy or a girl, Bosa?"

"It's a boy, Mama." Her hands shook and tears swelled in her eyes.

"Someone to take *Tata's* place in the world," Milka sighed.

"What, Mama?"

"Nothing, child, nothing. Tell the others to come and see their new brother."

The shelling was more intense as the days passed. Sometimes planes—mostly Italian—passed overhead and strafed the nearby fields. Milka and the children hid under sheets so that they would blend in with the snow.

On the fourth day, as the heavy guns came nearer, Milka was beside herself trying to nurse the baby and feed the children and keep them warm, all the while moving, trying to hide from the enemy. As soon as this wave of battle subsided, she would head for the caves in the hills. Or maybe even go home, if it were temporarily safe.

Home. Home without Lazo. He would never see his new son. He would never burst into the door and have six squealing children surround him. He would never bend his tall form to kiss her forehead again. *I must not think of this or I will go crazy; I must think of the children.* Food was running out. Soon, Milka would need to take one of the older children with her to try to find food. Fortunately, they had melted snow to drink.

With the constant noise of far-away shells and gunshots, in the agony of losing her Lazo and not being able to share it with the children yet, and with the demands of a newborn, Milka was overwhelmed and found it difficult to think. Yet by some miracle, she remembered a smoked ham she had buried near the house in the fall for just such possible dire circumstances. Cabbages were also hidden in a barrel in the far corner of the barn.

Late in the afternoon, as the sunset began to enclose them in the forest and the sound of the big guns was less intense, Milka gave orders to the children. "Bosa, you take care of the baby, and make sure none of the others moves from this spot unless shells start flying. The rest of you, stay in your quilts and don't move. Listen to Bosa. No fighting. No squabbling. No running around. Vaso, come with me."

"Yes, Mama," said Vaso, as he scrambled to his feet.

Milka moved quickly away from the children so she wouldn't change her mind about going. How hard it was to leave them unprotected. "*Bože moj! Please keep them safe till I return,*" she prayed. "*And please keep me safe to come back to them.*" With her bulk lightened by the delivery of the child four days earlier, she and Vasa moved quickly through the forest towards home. Explosions that seemed closer than before broke the lull in the shelling that had been so welcome to her before she left.

"We'd better hurry, Vaso," said Milka, picking up the pace." Seems like the fighting is getting closer.

"Mama, I have to go to the bathroom," Vaso complained.

"Now?" Milka stopped short and turned.

"Yes, Mama. I'm scared, and my stomach is sick and I have to go all the time." Vaso held his stomach and hopped from foot to foot.

"Okay. I'll keep walking, and when you're done, run and catch up with me. I'll take the usual route."

Milka hurried along to be able to quickly return to the children. Her full breasts leaked milk, which froze on her blouse as she rushed through the tangle of dark trees. "Oh, what misery!" she said, as she sank into a hole and fell, picked herself up again, and began running.

All of a sudden, as if a meteor shower suddenly burst from the heavens, the forest was lit bright red around her. Trees grew a hundred feet in her eyes and broke to surround her. Deafening booms split her eardrums. Then a pain so intense seared her body that she screamed like a wounded lioness, fell to the ground and remembered nothing more.

When she finally woke, her older children and a screaming baby surrounded her. "Mama! Mama! What shall we do?" Dazed, and with pain knifing through her body, she reached for the baby. "Give me the boy. Bosa, open my coat and blouse. Children, get under the sheets so they don't see you. The planes will come again."

She shook her head as she nursed the baby. "My God, can it get any worse? Bosa, tell me what happened. I cannot even move. I'm burning up even in this freezing temperature. Where am I? How did I get here?"

"We are not too far from home, Mama, but we cannot get there because they are fighting nearby. You're badly hurt. I tried my best. I tore a sheet and put it over the hole in your leg. There's a big piece of metal in there. It's still bleeding a lot, but it's not gushing like it was before. And you have lots of little pieces of metal in your back. I folded a sheet and put it there to absorb the blood. Mama, you are hurt badly, but please don't die. I don't know what to do."

"Who brought me here?"

"Vaso. After the shelling stopped, he ran to look for you. He dragged you all the way here."

"Oh my God, children! What you have to suffer. Where is he now?"

"He ran home to Srb to try and find help and maybe some food. Mama, the kids are so hungry." Bosa sobbed.

Milka could barely hold the baby any longer. Swirls kept dancing in and out of her mind. Her body felt as if it didn't belong to her anymore.

She wanted to dig deeper into the ground where she lay, to just give up, to burrow into the soil and maybe go underground somewhere to join Lazo. But the suckling at her breast forced her back to reality: if she didn't survive, neither would the children. She panted to try to get her voice back. "Bosa, take the baby. I think he's asleep." The last thing she heard before she drifted into a black cloud was shouting and the pops of gunfire.

When Milka woke she was warm, surrounded by a soft light in familiar surroundings. Everything was quiet. She must have died and gone to heaven. *God is good. He makes heaven look like your own home.* Then a swish of wind blew over her and she heard shouts.

"Vaso, hurry up. Bring the milk. Bring the kids in from the barn. They'll freeze. And we need more firewood."

A clatter of falling wood and the shouts of children made Milka realize that she wasn't dead, that she was alive and in her own home. *Oh, Bože moj! I made it. Thank you, Lord.* She pinched herself to make sure, then she called, "Children, come to your mother."

When the excitement died down, Bosa explained what had happened. "After you passed out, Vaso arrived with the Partisans from the village. He had found a Dr. Batas treating soldiers in the fields behind our house where the close fighting was going on between our men and the Italians

Milka Radjenović sitting at her kitchen table at her home in Srb.

Milan Prijić meeting his sister, Milka Radjenović for the first time in 1977. Milan left for the United States before she was born.

and Germans. He begged Dr. Batas to come to help you. The doctor said it would be impossible to come till he tended to the wounded in the field, but Vaso begged and cried so hard that the doctor said he would leave his assistant in charge and come to treat you. But he said he had to do it quickly because the wounded needed him. So he came with about five other guys, Partisans, and when he kneeled down to help you, then Nikola, our far neighbor, said they shouldn't help you because *Tata* is a Royalist. But the other guys—Djordje, Savo, and Ilija—told him to shut up and asked the doctor to go ahead.

After a short time, the doctor said he'd have to get you somewhere where he could operate. The men put you in quilt and carried you back to the house. Mama, Dr. Batas operated on you at the kitchen table while we all watched from the corner. The troops had already gone through, so he told us what to do for you and told us to stay in our own home because he said the battle had moved on.

After he finished, he washed his hands of the blood and patted each of us kids on the head 'You have any *šlivovitz*?' he asked. I got some from where you hide it in the back room. He drank the *rakija*, took one last look at you and said 'God help you and your mother, children' and left us."

"How long ago was that?" Milka shook her head and tried to orient herself to the fuzz of her mind and the pain of her body.

"About five days ago. I've been sponging you off ever since and trying to change and dry your sheets, and keep your bandages clean like Dr. Batas told me. Do you want to see the bunch of shrapnel he took out of your body, Mama? He said if you survived you would have lots of scars."

And survive she did. From the time she got on her feet again after her near fatal injuries, Milka determined she would never leave home, regardless of what fate dealt her. She would defend her family from her front door.

When a German unit came through towards the end of the war, pounding on the door and demanding that she give them all the food she had, she simply said "No. I must feed my children." She clutched her only chicken tightly in her arms, as the kids hid behind her full form. "Give me that chicken, woman," a young soldier said.

"No, you will have to kill me first.

The young soldier raised his pistol and pointed it in Milka's face, only to be grabbed at the wrist by his superior officer. "Leave her alone. We will go elsewhere." In the eyes of the officer Milka saw a weariness and pain that were perhaps equal to what he saw in her eyes. "I have a wife and children myself, lady. I hope I find them at home when the war is over."

Milka's children always hoped that one day it would be their father who came through the front door, but Milka—to spare them even more pain—hid from them the fact that their father was never coming back. In the spring, when the pink buds on the plum trees began to appear, and the snow melted into the mud puddles in the yard, she decided it was time to tell them the truth.

"Children, your father is not coming home. He was shot and killed by the Germans on Christmas Eve." Milka thought she had braced herself for the crying and the sadness, but when the accusing eyes of the children confronted her, it was almost too much to bear.

"It's not true, Mama. You're just joking with us, right?"

"Mama, you made that up, didn't you? *Tata* will be riding home on his horse one day and bringing us some food and oranges and maybe some walnuts, right?"

"If it were true, Mama, you would have told us earlier," said Vaso. "My *Tata* will be coming home."

"No, children, I am not lying. I almost died myself when I heard it just before we had to run to the forest. I didn't believe it. But the men of the village who were with *Tata* confirmed it. We must find out where he is buried and bring him home."

After much crying and lamentation, the children realized that their mother was telling the truth. When Milka found out from the other men how far away Lazo had fallen and been buried, and considered how long he'd been dead, she decided to leave him where he lay. On the first warm day of spring, she and the children trudged through the mud making a pilgrimage to the gravesite. Vaso had carved a headstone out of wood, marking the date of birth and death and the name Lazo Radjenović. Each child laid a prized possession on top of their father's grave. Then the small dejected group, heads down, led by a mother with a tiny baby cuddled in her arms, walked back home.

In 1978, Milka visited America. My sister Angelia and her friend Jim
went to JFK International Airport in New York to pick her up. Signals got
mixed up and Angelia and Jim were late. They decided to page Milka and
hoped that she was still at the gate.

When they got to the gate, she was waiting, but confused by the
paging over the speaker system. She thought that it was God calling her.

We had a grand time with *Tetka* Milka as she enjoyed seeing things
she had never dreamed of. We took her to Wisconsin Dells—a Midwest
playground—where she rode in an Old West stagecoach and on an
amphibious vehicle called the "Duck" that traveled from the parking
lot into a river. She was stunned.

Never a woman to be stationary, Milka decided to weed the garden
at our home. She found a rake and some diggers in the garage and
proceeded to work. I noticed that she had on her best green dress, a dress
that her daughters had made especially for the trip. I went outside to ask
if perhaps she might not want to change into something more casual. She
said, "This is the dress they made me for my journey to America. When I
get back, I'll never wear it again. I should save the clothes I need to wear."

One day, Milka walked through the house pounding the walls. She
moved between the kitchen and the family room and pounded the
wall that separated the two rooms. The wall sounded hollow because it
contained a sliding door. "Do you still know the name of your carpenter?"
she asked.

"Why?" I asked.

"Because he cheated you on this wall," she said. "It shakes when
you pound it. I would call him back and make him do the wall over."

I showed her the sliding door, but she still wasn't convinced. In her
village, the walls were made of thick cement, and she couldn't understand
why in America where they were supposed to have the best, the walls
were not solid.

Milka loved seeing her older brother, my father Milan, his family, and
America but was very happy to get home to her little, solid home and her
big family. Her children—all educated and successful—adored her and
felt a great loss when she died.

Vukašin (Djuro, George) Prijić

"When I walked down Wisconsin Avenue in my uniform, the girls fainted in the streets," Uncle George said when he showed us kids his World War II army pictures. "I was the best damn good-looking guy in the whole United States Army."

And he was handsome, with his piercing blue eyes and fine physique—quite a ladies' man, Arthur Murray dance lessons and all. You'd never guess that he was a village boy and had married at age fifteen.

When my dad, Milan, and his brother, Rade, emigrated to the United States, Uncle George was left as the oldest brother at home in Srb. Grandpa Ilija died sometime in the late 1920s, and shortly after that, his second wife also died. According to village custom, it was George's responsibility to take care of his younger brothers and sister. So at age 15, George was forced to pick a wife to move into the family home and take care of the remaining eight children.

The Feast of the Virgin Mary in August is the traditional time for young men and women to dress in their village best and come to the festival to see and be seen. After the tough days of planting and tending crops, and before the harvest, the Feast of the Virgin Mary (*Velika Gospojna*) offered a day of roast lambs on the spit,

George Prijić as a private in the United States Army in World War II.

gossip, and *kolo* dances. On this feast day, George was instructed by his family to choose a bride, one that would be competent enough to raise a family.

"My relatives took me around, and we talked about all the different young ladies," Uncle George said. "Then I saw a beautiful girl with pink cheeks and a long black braid, and she smiled at me, and my heart stopped. I knew she was the one." Uncle George sighed. "But it was not to be.

"What happened is there was another young lady, around 25, who had a necklace of gold coins around her neck, and my uncles said I must choose her because she was richer. And that was Mika. I never married the one I really wanted."

Mika was a quiet and obedient wife to George and a good mother to the other kids, but the marriage was not particularly happy and there were no children.

In 1938, my father Milan brought Mika and George to America. The young couple looked around, and with Milan's help, tried to fit in and make a go of it. George loved it, but Mika didn't, and after eleven months, she decided to go back to Srb. George stayed.

In 1941, when the United States joined the war effort against the Nazis in Germany, George Prijić, recent immigrant, was inducted into the U.S. Army. An infantryman, he was a part of General George Patton's army and a part of the invasion of Normandy and the Battle of the Bulge.

He didn't like Patton, although he admired his courage. "We grunts hid in the back when Patton came," Uncle George said. "He was mean; he liked to spot you out and yell at you."

George didn't talk much about the misery of war. He was there on Normandy when his buddies were shot down like ducks in a shooting gallery, their blood turning the ocean to waves of red. He was there walking past piles of dead German and American soldiers at the Battle of the Bulge, the acrid stench of death filling his nostrils.

"I got ordered to the rear detachment, the clean-up job," he said. "We had to take care of snipers and stragglers. We stayed behind, and it got colder and colder as the winter approached." Uncle George bemoaned the fact that he didn't have a proper uniform, coat or boots to take him into the winter months. "I knew if I didn't do something, I'd lose my legs. So when things were quiet, I looked for some shelter at night."

What saved George were the haystacks in the barns where, in off-duty hours, he covered himself with straw. "Thank God I was a farm boy and knew that the straw would keep me from freezing to death." As it happened, George suffered permanent damage to his legs, the after effects he was to feel the rest of his life. For his bravery in combat, he received several medals, medals he never got until just two years before his death.

Rumor had it that when George had leave during the war, he'd come to Milwaukee, check into a hotel without letting my dad know he was in town and call all his married and unmarried lady friends on 2nd Street to let them know they could visit him at the hotel anytime. After a week or so, he'd call my dad and say, "Hi Bro, I just got into town and I'm coming over."

After the war, perhaps as an antidote to the pain, or to get better use of his legs, he took Arthur Murray dance lessons. He used to tell us kids of the fun times he had dancing at the Eagle's Ballroom in Milwaukee, how beautiful the chandeliers and the ladies were, and how much he enjoyed dancing with the women. Then he'd say, "Well, I gotta go take a shave now," and put on tons of aftershave, get dressed in his best suit, and place the natty straw hat that was part of his everyday look at a jaunty angle on his head.

He often lived at our small house on 2nd and Madison when he was between jobs, and after his own grocery store failed. After a while he moved to San Jose, California, where he got a job as a butcher for a veterans' hospital.

Sometime in the late 1940s, George had divorced Mika. Even so, she continued to live in the Prijić family home in Srb. When we went to Srb on visits, she told us of the five armies that had gone through the village during World War II—German, Italian, Croatian *Ustashe, Chetnik* Royalists, Tito's Partisans—and how the villagers suffered under each and every one in varying degrees.

The safest places to hide were in the caves in the hills. The villagers hid there for five years while the various armies marched through. Mika sneaked home at night to scrounge for food or to gather goods to keep warm in the dark winter nights in the caves. Mika protected the family home as well as she could.

When Uncle George retired, with a disability pension from the American government and his Social Security, he went back to live in Srb with Mika. He was rich by local standards and gave a lot to friends and relatives around him. Mika took care of him, and he of her, when he wasn't off on the Yugoslav coast dancing under the moonlight with the foreign ladies who vacationed there.

"I'm the most popular guy in all of Opatija," he used to tell us. "The German ladies just love to dance with me." I believe they did.

Meantime, Mika in her black scarf and simple, dark dress, cooked and cleaned for him, and when we visited she made "American breakfast" of ham and eggs for us. "Please," she asked me one time, "the next time when you come, can you bring one of those things that turns the eggs over so I don't break them? George likes what you call 'over easy.'"

But she died before I had a chance to bring the spatula. Uncle George took care of her until her last day.

Uncle George received his medals from WWII
just two years before he died in 1992.

Uncle George wasn't so lucky. His dying days were during the Balkan wars of the 1990s and his pension checks and medication were held up by an American embargo on goods going to Serbians. So he died a miserable death from stomach cancer, without benefit of painkillers, but fortunately under the care of a kind next-door neighbor who washed, changed, and fed him. Let's hope there was enough *šlivovitz* to kill some of the pain.

And let's hope he received the letter from all of us—the relatives in Milwaukee—that said how much we loved him, and how much he meant to us.

Vojislav (Voja) and Fedora (Dora) Vojvodić

Uncle Voja was our mother's youngest brother and our favorite of all the uncles on Mom's side. He was spirited, funny, and spoke excellent English.

For a year in the 1960s, while we were teenagers, he lived with us in Milwaukee. He belonged to the church choir and hung out with the three of us girls at Leon's Custard Stand, Big Boy, the drive-in movies, and high school football games. He always said it was the best year of his life.

Voja was raised by Mika and Miljan Vojvodić in Srb village. His brother, Miljan, realized that this young and sensitive boy was very intelligent, so although Voja had chores around the farm, Miljan made sure he finished his studies every day. And it paid off: Voja won a scholarship for bright, orphaned boys and had his high school, college tuition, and living expenses paid for by a wealthy man who had no children of his own.

Voja finished his education in Subotica, Yugoslavia. Afterwards, when he came back to Srb, Miljan wouldn't allow him to stay. "You are the educated one, Voja. Go and make something of yourself."

During World War II, Voja was a prisoner of the Germans and was made to do forced labor in a factory in Austria. Serbian captives were not allowed into air raid shelters and had to fend for themselves— above ground—during air raids. Voja felt it was a miracle that he survived.

In Subotica, after the war, Voja met the love of his life, Fedora Klajić— Aunt Dora. Here is their story in Aunt Dora's own words. She recounts it 54 years later, during yet another war in Yugoslavia. Her story has been translated into English.

Brothers Voja and Peran Vojvodić
in Srb, circa 1989.

August 17, 1999

Dear Miki,

The time is now 5 p.m. We have been without electricity more than three hours. A little earlier the announcer on the shortwave radio said that we'd be without electricity for another hour and a half. The bombing has stopped for now but the other problems are still with us. Everything is so expensive and most of the time we have no electricity. Everybody is worried about what they are going to do when the winter comes and we have no heat. Most of the newer homes have no chimneys and wood stoves like I have, so they depend on the electricity. I am so lucky to have the means to buy a little wood for my stove. The first thing anybody does when they receive money from abroad is buy wood, for we are afraid there will be a shortage.

I didn't freeze any vegetables or other food this year; I would only be nervous that it would all spoil without electricity. I hope to buy some canned vegetables at the store or maybe I can preserve some myself. Besides the bombings, the weather has been horrible, and there is rain all the time. The farmers are afraid that the potatoes will rot in the ground and that would be a terrible disaster, for if we have potatoes we can survive the winter. Much bad luck fills our lives now and I fear the same is true for the future.

This war has done as much to destroy us psychologically as physically. During the last six weeks, I have lost four close friends, one being Jovan, the husband of my dear friend, Jelka. In earlier times, four of us couples were inseparable, doing everything together. Now there are only four widows left. The burial will be on Friday in the town of Šabac, where Jovan is originally from, and then Jelka will move back there, and I will lose her also. What hurts me deeply is that I won't be able to attend the funeral in Šabac. One of our friend's sons has a car, but there was no way he could find gas, not even on the black market. The situation was the same when Voja died and many friends who lived out of town couldn't make it for his funeral. A dentist friend of mine said that he would try very hard to find gasoline within the next few weeks for I promised Jelka that, by all means, I would attend the 40-day memorial service for Jovan. I hope I can.

But now, as you have asked me, I will think of another time and tell you Voja's and my "love story." I think this is what you call it in English:

"I met Voja just after World War II and 'liberation,' as it was called by the communists. Before Voja, I had a boyfriend who was a veterinarian, although I don't think he ever finished his studies because the war interfered. He was mobilized by the Communist troops to be a veterinarian for army horses. He hadn't written for a long time, so I decided to go to the village where he was from to see if his family had any news because so many soldiers had died in the war.

I was traveling by train with my friend Ruža who was going to visit her aunt. Suddenly, two young gentlemen stepped into our coach. One of them was Ruža's friend from school and the other was Voja. The date was March 23rd, 1945.

We chatted and laughed and had a very good time, and when we left the train and headed in different directions, Voja walked with Ruža and asked her many questions about me. She told him that I was going to the village to find out about my boyfriend and he said, "Why does she need a boyfriend from so far away when there are so many interesting young men in her own hometown?"

After a few months, my boyfriend, Rajko, returned from the war and came to Subotica with the cavalry. At this time Subotica was under the jurisdiction of the military command because the military authority controlled the whole region.

I was assigned to be a teacher in a neighboring village, but because I was the only teacher and all around were soldiers—ours, Russian, Bulgarian—I was afraid to stay alone in the school building at night. So, every afternoon I returned back to Subotica.

In the evenings in Subotica—if possible—I would take a walk along the river with Rajko. This promenade was the custom among the young people in Yugoslavia. But every time we walked the promenade, so did Voja.

Voja was very persistent. He was always walking behind us, making comments, with the friend we met on the train. It seems that Voja decided from the first moment he saw me that he would try and win me over. People from Srb are very persistent and self-assured and in the long run, Voja succeeded.

After several months, I split with Rajko because I discovered he had another girlfriend and that offended me. Our courtship ended.

As soon as Voja discovered this news, he turned up wherever I went. Whenever I came from the village in the afternoon, he was waiting at the streetcar station. In the evenings, we walked along the paseo, and very soon he declared he wished to marry me.

At this time, everything was more formal, so he first paid a visit to my parents and asked for my hand in marriage. On the 23rd of March, 1946, exactly one year after we met on the train, our engagement party took place in my parents' home in the presence of a priest. Voja was very religious; he was a member of the church and the choir. One year he was even the kum (sponsor) for the Slava or Patron Saint's Day of the church. We got married on the 23rd of April.

Voja had an apartment, so after the wedding, I was to move there with him. At this time, we couldn't travel anywhere far away, so we went on a so-called honeymoon to

Belgrade. My cousin worked in a Belgrade hotel, and he was able to reserve one room for us at the Hotel Moskva. After the church wedding, we left, but we could not go directly to Belgrade, so we had to spend a night in a hotel in Novi Sad. On the second day, we went to Belgrade.

When we got to the Hotel Moskva, we explained who had made the reservations. The receptionist asked if we were on a honeymoon. We replied "Yes," so he laughed said he guessed that we only needed one bed then.

The next morning, we heard knocking on the door. We thought they were bringing us breakfast. An official from the hotel came to tell us that we had to remain in our room because the First of May celebration was taking place on the main square and Tito was going to speak. Therefore, every window looking onto the square had to be secured. A young soldier had entered with the official, and he placed himself next to the window and we had to stay in bed.

Whenever a soldier would leave for a minute, another soldier would enter. Maybe they knew that we were newlyweds and this was very interesting for them. So, in the first days of my marriage, I had a military guard. As you see, a person lives through many things in life, so in old age, at least he or she has some souvenirs.

After one week, we returned to Subotica. Voja continued to work in his bookstore. He didn't want me to go every day to the village to teach, so I resigned.

In 1952, I got another school position, and I started my studies of French and Serbian languages and literature in Novi Sad. I became a part-time student. It was difficult because I was working, but I passed my exams regularly.

French was not so popular at the time because everybody had to learn Russian. However, I graduated in French and have always loved the language and literature. I used the French language only later when I traveled to France.

My paternal uncle was in the French army and my
grandmother told me that when he died, he was buried as
a French soldier with other French soldiers in the city of
Čačak. My generation was somehow brought up in the spirit
of friendship, love, and respect for France and their people.
Even in World War II we were great allies with France,
so now I feel sorry that, in this present senseless war, we
distanced ourselves from each other.

During the first years of our marriage we vacationed at
the Rogaška Spa in Slovenia because Voja had a problem
with his stomach. Therapy in the spa was very good for him
and everything settled down. When we finally started to get
passports to travel in foreign countries—and particularly
when we got the inheritance from Uncle Grbić—in America—
we started to travel outside the country. This was a great
pleasure for us.

As far as our marriage is concerned, it was like any other
marriage. Everything was generally good, so thanks to God,
we spent 47 years together. Regardless of what happened in
our marriage, it is now quite difficult for me with Voja gone
and not having any children. Children mean a lot in the
life of their parents and particularly later when one of the
parents is left alone. Now when I have reached old age and
loneliness, I look at many things with different eyes. When
person is young, everything seems more beautiful.

In 1947, the Communist authorities confiscated Voja's
bookstore: nobody had a right to own his own business. So
Voja went to work in an import-export business. He knew
German well, which was a rare thing at the time. He also
started to learn English. He was very determined to learn,
and you, Miki, know how well he learned, since he wrote to
you in English.

This is the main outline of our life from the beginning to
the end. Now I am left alone so I think about many things

and look at my old photos and slides. So, I relive many things, and am so happy that we did all this so that now in old age I have nice memories. I've always loved Paris very much. Now I look at the book Promenades in Paris. Often, I take this book and read some parts, and so again I relive the streets, plazas, and museums that I so enjoyed in the past.

Voja was saying before he died that since we couldn't go to Opatija any more, since the Croatians had confiscated our property, we would try to go one more time to Paris. Poor guy didn't dream of how things would get messed up. He didn't know that he would go away for all time so soon. I am at least content that I am still in my own house, and despite everything, I can live quietly in my home, although not without worries and problems.

This awful, senseless war hit all of us, but particularly older people, and we are all suffering the consequences. It is terrible that at the end of my life, I cannot spend it in peace with the minimum of what I need. The best for me now is when I have something good to read or when I watch American and Mexican soap operas. At least it takes my mind off unpleasant things.

I think maybe I will try and go to the market when the bombs aren't falling so I can maybe find something to can. At least this won't spoil if I don't have electricity.

Tomorrow we should have the first pontoon bridge across the Danube. This should be particularly helpful for people who live in Srem and work in Novi Sad. These people have been crossing the river in rowboats. Yesterday I passed the Danube by bus; it was terrible to see the rows and rows of people waiting to cross.

I am very happy through all this bombing that my apartment hasn't been destroyed because many people in my neighborhood are left without roofs over their heads. At least I have electricity some of the time and my friend

promised to buy me a butane stove for cooking. I heard that
in Hungary they have this instant soup that you shake the
packet into a cup and just pour hot water in and voila you
have soup. Maybe when someone goes to Hungary, they can
bring me back some of those.

Even though I have aches and pains, I am very happy
that I can get around well enough for a woman of 77 years.
Whenever I have pain, I take your special medicine ADVIL,
and I feel much better. Many younger people have died
here, and I also see what happens in your country. I watch
Chicago Hope, which is my favorite show, and I see that
many of your young people die also.

Thank you so much for your help and for caring for me.

Love,

Aunt Dora

*Voja and Dora Vojvodić enjoying
a celebratory dinner in 1989.*

Uncle Voja died in 1995 during the Bosnian War in which the Croatian army almost totally destroyed his native village of Srb, Lika. At the time of his heart attack, he was living in Novi Sad, his home for many years. He was taken to the intensive care unit at Novi Sad Hospital where he died a week later. Aunt Dora was not allowed to visit due to a strict rule that no one is allowed to visit the intensive care patients. Since there was a shortage of medication due to sanctions put on Serbia by the Western allies, we can speculate that Voja died a very uncomfortable death.

Aunt Dora is still alive in a nursing home in Novi Sad. She has been in bed for over nine years since she was denied back surgery due to her age. Because of the intense pain she experienced when attempting to move, she permanently stayed in bed to assuage the pain. Consequently, her legs atrophied.

I saw Dora in 2016 at the nursing home. Physically, she was a fraction of the size she had been in the apex of her life and my cousin Sasha had warned me that she was often confused. A nurse guided us to Dora's bedside and woke her. The nurse put her arm around my aunt's shoulder and said, 'Dora is our longest living and favorite patient.' The other four women in the clean but small room listened intently, probably wondering which of them was going to be the next to leave. "Dora, Miki is here," the sympathetic nurse said. "She and her husband came to see you."

Dora smiled a beautiful, almost beatific smile. She listened to the conversation in the room and looked at the fruit and gifts we brought. After several minutes, the nurse asked Dora if she knew who I was. Not at all confused, she said, "That's my Voja's sister's daughter from America."

Aunt Dora died in her sleep in December of 2018. I had seen her in October. She didn't speak anymore, but we made eye contact when she woke and she smiled. I'm sure she recognized me.

Ilija (Eli) and Eleanor Prijić

Lying on their backs, smoking homemade cigarettes and looking up at the Julian Alps, two young boys, Vukašin (George) and Ilija (Eli) Prijić, talked of their dream of going to the United States. For most young boys in Srb, this would have been an impossible dream, but Vukašin and Ilija already had a brother, Milan, in America. Maybe one day Milan would make enough money to pay for their ship passage to the country of dreams.

"Pass another cigarette, Djuro."

"No, Ilija, we're out of cigarette paper and we need the rest of our book to study."

Since Djuro and Ilija were poor young teens and couldn't afford cigarettes or cigarette paper, they used pages from their religious textbooks. Not the whole pages, just the margins and white space. Their priest-teachers had told them never to deface their textbooks, especially the photos of the saints. The boys therefore never cut out the photos of saints for fear that God would punish them. However, they did need their cigarettes and used the white areas. Tobacco they got from the bale droppings on the barn floor.

In 1933, the now young men sailed on the *Leviathan* to the U.S. They were accompanied by two young women, George's wife, Mika, and brother Milan's future wife, Milka Vojvodić.

Uncle Eli, Millie, and Uncle George.

Ilija became Eli and Djuro became George, thanks to immigration officials on Ellis Island. Three of these immigrants immediately became students at the Milwaukee Technical School. The fourth, George's wife, Mika, decided after eleven months to go back to Srb and to live there permanently.

Eli, the youngest, became the most Americanized. He went to school and worked different jobs, then in 1941 was inducted into the U.S. Army. There he picked up culinary skills and helped feed thousands of World War II soldiers. After he left the army, he continued in the culinary trade and was chef at a variety of restaurants in Milwaukee.

On one of his evenings out with George to the famous Eagles Club in Milwaukee, Eli met the beautiful Eleanor Mizgalski from northern Wisconsin. Handsome in his military uniform, he had the confidence to ask Eleanor to dance, first the jitterbug, then many slow dances till the end of the evening.

While George was flitting from woman to woman, Eli stayed with Eleanor until closing time at eleven. She was intrigued by his stories and wonderful sense of humor; he was smitten by her infectious laugh. From then on, they were a pair. They married in 1943 and afterward had two wonderful daughters, Linda & Diane.

Eli and Eleanor visited Srb with Uncle George on one of his sojourns back to the village. Eli was thrilled to be in the town he left so long ago, but Eleanor had a hard time not knowing the language and other things.

"People were very nice," she offered, "but there were too damn many bedbugs."

Eleanor Mizgalski

Eli Prijić

What Is Srb
Like Today?

Srb, Lika, Croatia

2019

Serbians still make up the majority of the population of about 300, but they're mostly older. Young people complain that there's nothing to do in Srb, and compared to today's entertainment-packed, technological society, that's true. Srb is basically the small village it always was.

Very few students start kindergarten in the old school. Grades 1–3 are the only grades taught there. Improvements to the school have been minimal: new windows, a small gym, a little playground out back. For grades 4–8, 13 students are bused to nearby Gračac.

A doctor from a larger city visits twice a week where he sees patients from both Srb and Gračac in the old medical building. Serious cases are transferred to Zagreb or other bigger cities.

Getting work outside of farming is very difficult in Srb. The once-busy Ličanka sweater factory was bombed out during the wars of the 1990s and has never been rebuilt. No replacement factory is planned for Ličanka, Srb's largest employer in the former Yugoslavia.

The only new building in Srb is the big police station in the center of town. Two small stores, two cafes, one self-service store and the tiny hotel

The Ličanka sweater factory—Srb's largest employer—was bombed out in the 90s wars. The factory was never rebuilt.

employ a few workers. A younger couple had bought the mobile grocery truck—Monaco—which they drove around the village with supplies for those for whom it was difficult to go to town. Unfortunately, the prices on products doubled and the grocery truck closed.

In nearby Lapac, a small forestry and wood-working business is trying to make a go of it, and there's some cheese-making by a few locals to send to the markets in larger cities. Several farmers are trying to start a business to ship Srb's abundant and delicious raspberries to larger markets, but they have not figured out a way to successfully transport the delicate fruit. Also, taxes on larger farms are very high, so local farmers have decided it's not worth it to grow crops except for themselves.

Several people from Srb have moved to Gračac to look for work in the larger town. They're trying to remodel homes that were abandoned after the war. However, if they didn't live in those houses during the war, they won't get any outside help from charities or the Croatian government.

Of my relatives, only Nikola, Miljan's son and his wife, Dušanka, live in Srb full-time, although they travel during the winter to see their children in Rotterdam or go to a spa for health purposes. Having worked

Dušanka Vojvodić as a young farm wife in Srb, 1958.

Dušanka in the front yard of her Srb home in 2008, after living and working in Rotterdam for over 25 years.

in Rotterdam for many years as guest workers, they both have good pensions. They remodeled the damage done when their home in Srb was looted by the Croatian army. They now have a lovely three-bedroom home with flower gardens, something rare in Srb.

Nikica Vojvodić, David's son, comes to Srb only in the spring. His bombed-out home was rebuilt by the Lutheran church charities. Some of Peran's family come to visit Srb in the warmer weather and one of Peran's grandsons lives in Srb.

However, when the word gets out that one of Srb's sons or daughters is visiting—like me—somehow people appear from nowhere with their open arms and warm hospitality and it's difficult to turn down the abundance of *šlivovitz*, *slatko*, chicken, lamb and fresh *pogača* offered. Srb springs to life again.

Addenda

Milan Prijić Returns to Srb

1977

Sixty years after Milan Prijić left Srb, Lika, Yugoslavia, he decided to go back for a visit. Six members of his American family accompanied him for this special occasion: 3 daughters, including me, a son-in-law, and two grandchildren.

We all met in the coastal town of Zadar, Croatia, because it had a direct train—a narrow gauge train called a *šinobus*—from Knin to Srb. The train was packed with workers headed home from their coastal jobs back to their villages for the weekend. By the time we boarded, the workers had already dipped into their *šlivo* supplies and were singing and telling wild stories mixed with juicy swear words and whoops.

Captivated by us and particularly with my dad, the workers wanted to know more about Milan's history. When they found out that Vukašin— Uncle George Prijić —was Milan's brother, the crowd went wild. Suitcases stuffed with salami, cheese, fresh bread, boiled eggs, and tomatoes and peppers were flipped open, plates appeared, and all travelers in the train car were served a grand picnic.

Uncle George, with his white straw hat, sparkling white shirts and colorful American ties, was a frequent traveler on the *šinobus*. The young men admired his generosity, charm and his ability to attract well-to-do foreign ladies.

We reached Srb about 3 p.m. and when we got off, we were surprised to see an empty station. Even though we had sent Uncle George a telegram and affirmed with a phone call to the post office when we were arriving, a welcoming committee was not there to greet us.

George Prijić standing behind Djuro Vojvodić with Miki's husband, Ivan Knezević.

Where was Djuro Americanac?

We waited for about 20 minutes and then the local mailman, Marjan, stepped up and offered to take us to Uncle George's house in his mail truck. Lacking another option, we piled into the back of the van and sat sandwiched on wooden benches among the bags of mail. My dad was lucky enough to find a seat alongside the driver.

Bumping up and down a dirt road trying to avoid barrel-sized pot holes, Marjan looked over at Milan and asked, "What do you think of Srb so far?"

"Well, I haven't seen too much yet," answered Milan, "but I can tell you one thing, the roads haven't changed at all."

A roar of laughter came from the back of the truck as we bounced along the way.

Just before crossing the railroad tracks, Marjan slammed on the brakes. The gates were down and a line of cars waited on the opposite side of tracks. Next to the lead car was a tall man in a white straw hat: Uncle George. "We were on the way to the station and Vaso stopped us and said that you had already gotten a ride in the mail truck. I guess the *šinobus* was early," George yelled.

Marjan stuck his head out the side window and shouted, "Don't you know we changed to the fall schedule last week? No one ever looks at the schedules around here." He shook his head and said, "Move out of the way. I have my passengers and mail to deliver. Special delivery."

Marjan gunned the engine and Uncle George raised the gates.

"See you at your house," said Marjan, waving. "Make a U-turn and follow me!"

One morning, several days after the family's arrival, Milan was sitting on the porch having fresh brown bread, plum jam, basa and coffee. He was enjoying his conversation with his brother and former sister-in-law, Mika.

People on the way to work or going to the small village store stopped by to see the American guests and especially Milan. Looking up the road, we saw a small man walking towards us. His step was lively even though he used a cane. He wore a red Lika cap and a heavy brown sheepskin vest, typical of the peasant apparel of the area. He stopped in front of the house and greeted us all.

"Would you like a glass of water?" Mika asked him.

"Yes, daughter, that would be fine. I've been walking quite a way." He wiped his sweaty forehead.

"How far did you walk?" asked Milan.

"About 6 kilometers," he said. "From the top of that mountain."

"Wow," said Milan. "I couldn't do it."

The visitor laughed and looked at Milan. "So where have you been, son?" he asked. "I haven't seen you in a while."

My dad looked at him and said, "I've been in America for a while. Sixty years, in fact."

"I thought it must have been some time since I saw you last. When I heard you were visiting, I had to come down from the mountain to see you. Daughter, could you bring me a *šlivo* and coffee?"

"Yes, Father. Sit down. I'll bring it for you."

My dad's eyes opened wide and he looked at Mika. "This is your father, Šima?"

"Yes, I'm Šima. Ninety-six years old," he said, pounding his chest. "Son, you haven't changed a bit since you left. You look good."

"You too, Šima. Not at all."

We stayed in Srb for a week, dining with numerous relatives to the point of bursting from so much food and drink. In between meals, Milan took us on walks to show us where he tended his sheep and dreamed of owning his own store. He showed us his schoolhouse where he went for three years before he was forced to quit. He recounted a particular incident in which he had been beaten by his father for staying home from school when he was sick with fever. His father had believed the teacher/priest who said the boy was lazy, instead of Milan, who really was sick. Milan carried a grudge against the priest his entire life.

We walked with him in the fruit orchard and he showed us his favorite pear tree. The sweet, soft pears tasted as good to him as they had when he was a child. How great it was hearing stories of my dad's youth and reminiscing with him about his early years.

When all of us went back to Belgrade to meet with relatives and to say goodbye to part of the group that was leaving, two males who were particularly glad to be flying home were Milan and his grandson, Ivo Knezevic, 9. Upon seeing his grandfather, Ivo ran up to him and they shook hands vigorously and hugged. "We're going home, Grandpa," Ivo said.

"You bet," said Milan. "Aren't we lucky!"

Family toast with šlivovitz on the occasion of
Milan Prijič's visit to Srb after a 60 year absence.

Family Photo Album

Author, Miki, with cousin, Nikica Vojvodić in 1989.

Angelia Prijic Jovanovic and family with Uncle George at Sklop, the waterfall in Srb, 1989.

Gab session with Miki's family, Baba Soka and young neighbor girl in 1977.

*Cousin Nikola Vojvodić
with Miki in 2008.*

*Nikola Vojvodić roasts a lamb
in honor of the family's visit in 2008.*

*Uncle George Prijić's
former wife, Mika.
Circa 1977.*

Poetry by Angelia Prijic Jovanovic

Čemernica

Mountain called Sorrow,
From you I can almost see the sea,
Bright turquoise Adriatic
Beside the Karst Formations and Dinaric Alps.

We have come to the meadow to harvest hay,
That feeds the red mare and her colt in winter,
And the prolific cow Dikulja,
Who lives in the stall under the house.

It took four hours to get here for sunrise,
Walking by lantern light past Milka's bush,
The stand of shrubs within which my mother was born,
As her parents walked this way
From the winter home in the valley
To their summer home in the mountains.

No midwife,
Nikola helped birth his daughter, then,
Strong and proud, carried wife and child
And climbed to the home on Čemernica,
In time for the harvest.

I am here, generations later, for the harvest.
Drinking *slivovitza*, eating raw smoked bacon
And onions for breakfast.
Singing with cousins and neighbors,
Vibrato induced by echo,
Continuo by mountain streams.

I cannot stop seeing.
Everywhere I look has no end.
Viewed from the high mountain meadow,
The horizon blurs,
Direction becomes circumference,
Mist rises from the universe.

Freshly cut hay
Stacked vertically against tall poles to dry.
Golden fields, a sweet, sexy fragrance
Carried by heat and wind to heaven and earth.

Let me please lie here forever,
Arms held over my head in surrender
On the black earth that holds my ancestors,
Listening to the sounds of the meadow.

No. We leave before sunset
To descend on precarious paths,
Bells on the horse cart jingling
So those on foot can follow in the dark.
Until mega millions of stars awaken
To light the way from Čemernica,
This place I'll never be again.

Boja

Black, black hair,
flowing below your waist
when spilled free
from tight braids.

Beauty of the village,
bearer of eight children
whose tiny fingers surely twisted
its silkiness as they suckled.

Young mother,
when could you wash it with ash from *lipa* leaves,
brush it with pig bristle, perfume it with field flowers,
fill your husband's last breath with its scent?

Young widow, cover your hair
with a hot, black, homespun scarf.
sin and shame to tempt mourners
to lose themselves in the feel of it.

Pull it back from your eyes
as you bend to pound clothes clean
on smooth rocks of the mountain river
flowing cold through your legs.

Bind it tight as you scythe high mountain meadows of wheat,
tend to chickens and sheep,
oxen and horses and neighbors,
your children, alone, alone.

Exhausted. Dead at thirty-eight.
Hair black as darkness frames your cold face.
Your daughter's black, black braids
Shine wet with tears.

Ujaci

It was the last time they were pictured together,
standing at the door
of Peran's house in Lika,
the home THEY looted and burned.

Uncle Peran,
strong and brown as coffee,
make me dance again to the *kolo*
you play on your *frula*,
and we'll laugh when you pound your fist
on your stomach to show how tough you are,
tough enough to defy them to kill you–
and THEY did.

Uncle Voja,
light-hearted as laughter,
sing duets with me
in your nasal tenor voice.
Always pleasing, wait politely
for the last, smallest piece.
Wait until death, for just a little
of the U.S. boycott medicine
THEY forbid you to have.

Good-bye my mother's brothers
standing side by side at the door,
smiling at me forever as I took your picture,
unsuspecting of impending horror,
innocent victims of war.

*Angelia Prijic Jovanovic is a psychologist who recently retired as
a counselor at Sacramento City College in California. She and her
husband, Dragan Jovanović, have four children and two grandchildren. Angelia has visited Srb, Lika many times and through her
writing, one can intuit the love she has for her parents' birth village.
Her magnificent poetry speaks for itself.*

Acknowledgements

This book, *Srb, Lika, A portrait of a small village,* was a long time coming. Although the book had been written in rough draft, I was so involved in other projects that I didn't take the time to actually write this memoir until now.

The first trip with my mother to the village of her birth was an eye-opening experience. The travel was awesome: Milwaukee to New York by train; crossing the Atlantic to La Havre (Paris) by ship; France to Switzerland, Italy and finally Yugoslavia on the Simplon-Orient Express. The people I met and the differences in their lifestyles opened my eyes and heart to a grand experience that I never forgot.

I wish to thank many people who helped me along the way and hosted me over the years when I visited Srb.

For car trips around Yugoslavia, I am especially grateful to my cousin, Dr. Mira Andre, and her father, Djoko Pilipović. We traveled from Belgrade to Srb and around the northern Adriatic coast. Uncle Vojislav Vojvodić and Dora Vojvodić were particularly helpful to my mother and me. The Grbić, Vojvodić, Ivančević and Prijić families were also involved in hosting and traveling with us. Throughout the years, others assisted with transportation: Rastko Jurisić, Dr. Dusko Knezević, Anja Knezević, Dr. Ivan Knezevic, Sasha Dubajić. A special thanks to Jelka Saponjić and Sally Novakovic who sometimes accompanied me on my adventures.

For stories, I'd like to thank Milan and Milka Prijić, Vojislav and Dora Vojvodić, Angelia Jovanovic, George Prijić, Dušanka & Nikola Vojvodić, Nikica Vojvodić, Milica Vojvodić, Jelena Kurepa and Smilja Dubajić.

For editing and writing suggestions, I thank Anné Knezevic, Ivan Knezevic, Phil Hart, Mary Niklanovich Hart, Stacey Caplan and Judy Nystrom. To Alex Knezevic, many, many thanks for designing my website, mikikn.com

A special thank you to Phil Hart for drawing the informative maps of the region of Srb, Lika, in different time periods.

For photos, other than mine, I thank Dragan and Angelia Jovanovic and their children, Andrew, Milan, Martin and Adriana. Others who contributed are Daryll Michaelis, Linda Schneider and Ivan Knezevic.

For the beautiful book design, I wish to give special thanks to the inimitable, talented Stacey Caplan, who spent countless hours designing and combining the transcript and the photos. Thanks for your patience and the sharing of many cappuccinos!

I chose to limit the stories to the siblings of my mother and father, but there are hundreds more tales like theirs. Villages like Srb are disappearing around the world. This book gives a glimpse into a type of life that may never re-appear. People have left to escape ethnic fighting, to seek advanced education, to marry outside the village and to emigrate to other countries. Small farming doesn't pay and migration to larger cities for financial needs robs the villages of their young. While the majority of those remaining in villages like Srb are primarily aged, a recent trend is the return of former residents for short stays to celebrate holidays or help their elderly families work in the fields.

Živeli. Here's to good health and long life!

Delicious plums often end up as the Serbian national drink: šlivovitz.